everyday

simple
sophisticated
knitted
garments

Lace

heather zoppetti

INTERWEAVE
interweave.com

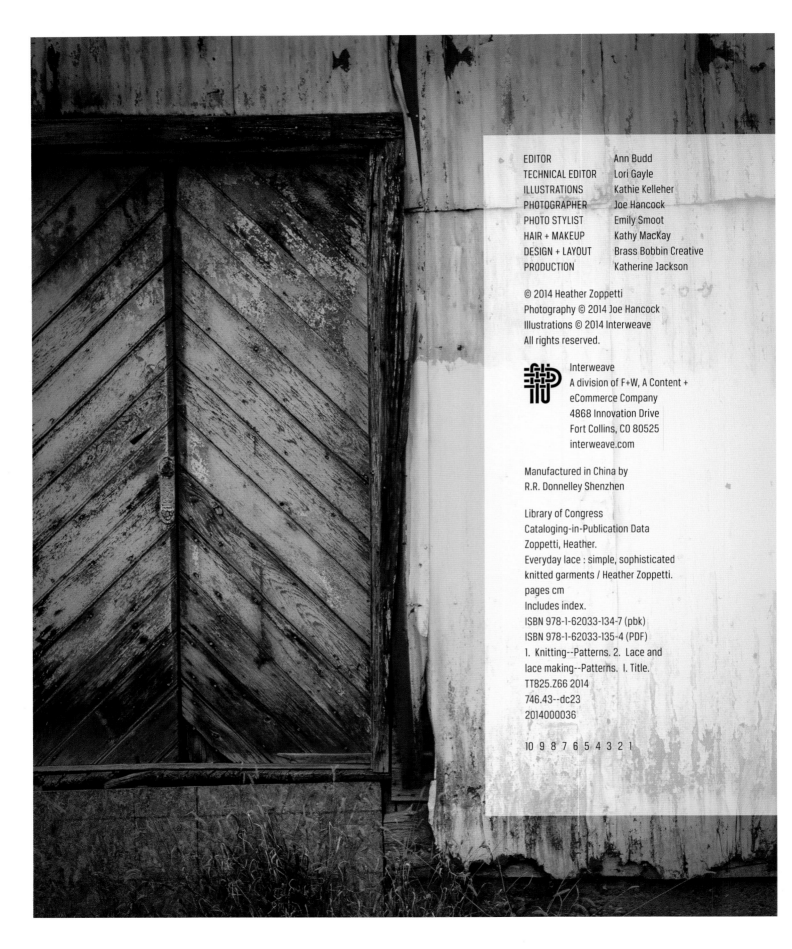

EDITOR   Ann Budd
TECHNICAL EDITOR Lori Gayle
ILLUSTRATIONS   Kathie Kelleher
PHOTOGRAPHER   Joe Hancock
PHOTO STYLIST   Emily Smoot
HAIR + MAKEUP   Kathy MacKay
DESIGN + LAYOUT   Brass Bobbin Creative
PRODUCTION   Katherine Jackson

Interweave
A division of F+W, A Content +
eCommerce Company
4868 Innovation Drive
Fort Collins, CO 80525
interweave.com

Manufactured in China by
R.R. Donnelley Shenzhen

Library of Congress
Cataloging-in-Publication Data
Zoppetti, Heather.
Everyday lace : simple, sophisticated
knitted garments / Heather Zoppetti.
pages cm
Includes index.
ISBN 978-1-62033-134-7 (pbk)
ISBN 978-1-62033-135-4 (PDF)
1. Knitting--Patterns. 2. Lace and
lace making--Patterns. I. Title.
TT825.Z66 2014
746.43--dc23
2014000036

10 9 8 7 6 5 4 3 2 1

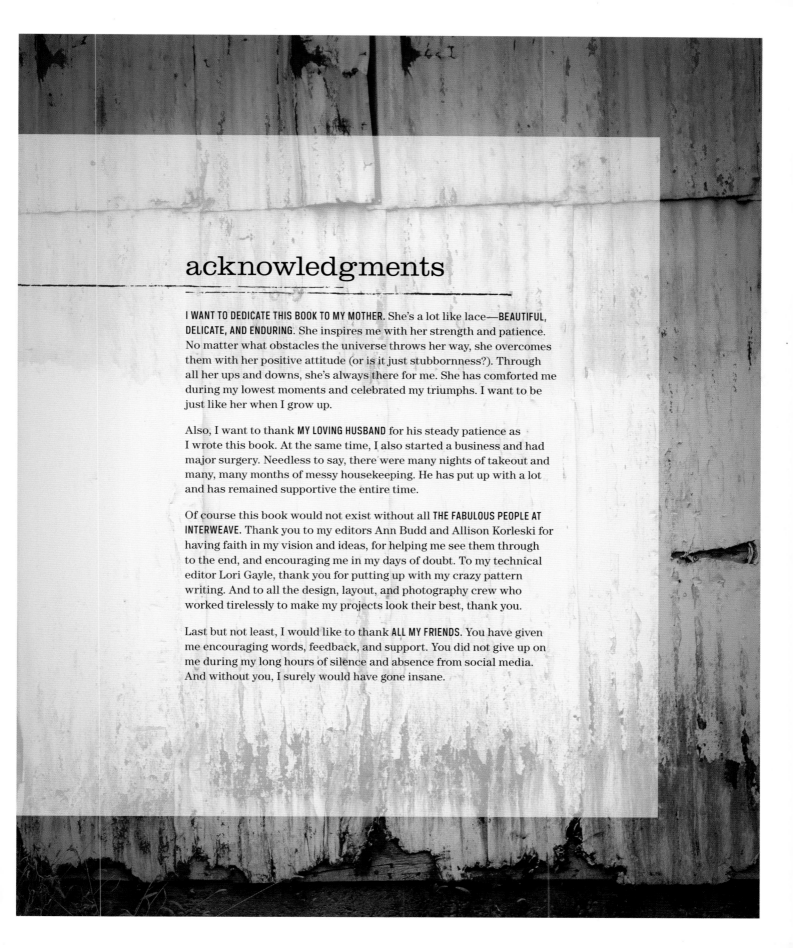

acknowledgments

I WANT TO DEDICATE THIS BOOK TO MY MOTHER. She's a lot like lace—BEAUTIFUL, DELICATE, AND ENDURING. She inspires me with her strength and patience. No matter what obstacles the universe throws her way, she overcomes them with her positive attitude (or is it just stubbornness?). Through all her ups and downs, she's always there for me. She has comforted me during my lowest moments and celebrated my triumphs. I want to be just like her when I grow up.

Also, I want to thank MY LOVING HUSBAND for his steady patience as I wrote this book. At the same time, I also started a business and had major surgery. Needless to say, there were many nights of takeout and many, many months of messy housekeeping. He has put up with a lot and has remained supportive the entire time.

Of course this book would not exist without all THE FABULOUS PEOPLE AT INTERWEAVE. Thank you to my editors Ann Budd and Allison Korleski for having faith in my vision and ideas, for helping me see them through to the end, and encouraging me in my days of doubt. To my technical editor Lori Gayle, thank you for putting up with my crazy pattern writing. And to all the design, layout, and photography crew who worked tirelessly to make my projects look their best, thank you.

Last but not least, I would like to thank ALL MY FRIENDS. You have given me encouraging words, feedback, and support. You did not give up on me during my long hours of silence and absence from social media. And without you, I surely would have gone insane.

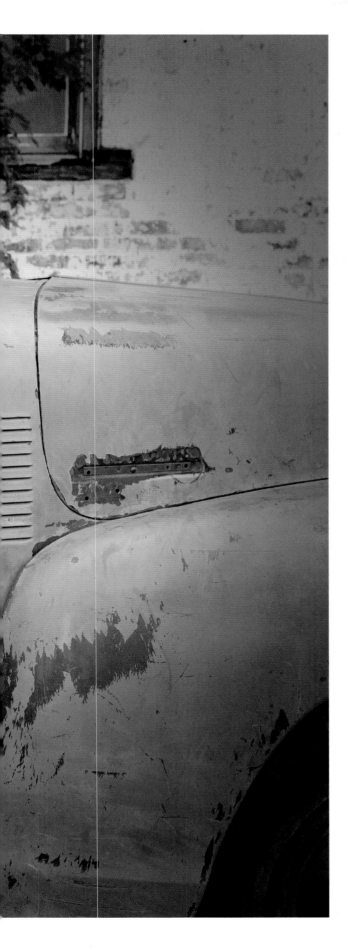

introduction

In college, when the Internet was young and Ravelry didn't exist, I started knitting. Along with my roommate, I bought those *I Can't Believe I'm . . .* booklets, cheap yarn, and long aluminum needles. During episodes of *Survivor,* I taught myself to cast on, to knit, and to purl. From there my hobby turned into an obsession: I wanted to knit everything, and I was fearless. My first projects included a basketweave scarf, a lace baby blanket, and a pair of socks. I didn't have anyone to tell me that these things were difficult, so they weren't.

As many do, I fell in love with lace at the very first stitch. I loved the way that just a few special stitches created breathtakingly beautiful patterns. It was only natural that I turned to lace when I started to design on my own. My popular Dahlia Cardigan (*Interweave Knits,* Fall 2011) celebrates my love of lace.

In recent years, lace shawls and lace-trimmed shawlettes have become wildly popular among knitters, especially those new to lace knitting. Although they're fun and knit up relatively quickly, I find that I rarely wear them. To me, they're a bit too fancy for everyday wear, and I pull them out only for special occasions or events where I know that my workmanship will be appreciated.

The projects in this book support my belief that lace should be liberated from its confinement to shawls and be incorporated into everyday garments and accessories. A bit of lace—be it a simple trim, a narrow panel, or an interesting edging—can bring sophisticated femininity to a wardrobe without overwhelming fussiness. To this end, I've relied on simple construction techniques that highlight the beauty of the lace patterns. The result is a collection of timeless classics that will hold their appeal year after year.

This book is divided into three sections based on the seasons—warm, transitional, and cold. Garments in the warm section include delicate knitted lace that's light and airy. The transitional section is filled with projects designed for the spring and fall months when simple layers and classic designs are most welcome. Thicker yarns, striking sweaters, and toasty accessories that focus on warmth and comfort complete the cold section. In short, you can enjoy a bit of lace every day of the year.

With knitters of all skill levels in mind, the projects in this book range from beginner to intermediate. The simplest patterns are a great introduction to lace knitting, and the more advanced projects will challenge experienced lace knitters. Wherever you fit in the spectrum, I hope that you'll find projects you'll want to knit and wear every day in *Everyday Lace!*

CHAPTER 1

Lace-Knitting
essentials

Lace is my favorite knitting technique—I find lace patterns fun to design and fun to knit. Very simply, lace is created by yarnovers, which create intentional holes in the knitting. To help define the yarnovers and to maintain a constant stitch count (and therefore width of fabric), every yarnover is typically paired with some type of decrease. The sequence and type of yarnovers and decreases can create a wide array of patterns.

To make the most of your lace knitting, you'll want to choose the right tools, become adept at reading charted patterns, and be diligent about blocking.

tools

Although you can use the same tools that you use for general knitting, you'll find things go more smoothly if you choose those that are particularly suited for lace patterns.

In most cases, you'll want to choose a **NATURAL-FIBER YARN** that can be blocked after the knitting is complete. Synthetic yarns do not stretch the same as natural fibers and will not hold the shape produced by blocking. Garments made from these yarns will always look the same as when they came off the needles. For the best results, be sure to use a yarn that contains a large percentage of natural fibers such as wool, silk, or cotton.

There are literally hundreds of **KNITTING NEEDLES** on the market today; how do you choose which to use for lace knitting? Like many tools, there are several tradeoffs to consider. Bamboo, plastic, and wooden needles have more surface texture that will help prevent the stitches from jumping off the needles. Bamboo and plastic have a softness that allows them to flex, which can be beneficial to arthritic hands. Metal needles can be tricky for slick yarns, such as cotton or linen, but they often have sharper points that make easy work of the various types of decreases involved with lace patterns. If you're new to lace knitting, you might find bamboo or wood needles with sharp points the ideal combination.

STITCH MARKERS can help you keep track of different sections in the knitting, and many of the projects in this book call for their use. However, you may find that placing a marker after every repeat of a lace pattern can lead to headaches. Not only will your progress be slowed by slipping multiple markers every row, but some patterns, such as the Manor Ridge Body chart (page 41), require that double decreases are worked on the last stitch of one repeat and the first stitch of the next repeat. You'll have to temporarily remove the marker to perform the double decrease, then return it in the proper place afterward. You may find it easier to use just two markers—one to mark the stitches before the beginning of the first pattern repeat and another to mark the stitches after the end of the last pattern repeat.

If you plan to follow a chart, you'll find that placing HIGHLIGHTER TAPE on the working row of a chart will help you keep your place. Simply move the tape from row to row as you knit.

ROW COUNTERS are nice for keeping track of which row in a pattern was last completed. There are many varieties of rows counters, including those that sit on the table, attach to your knitting needles, and even electronic apps for smart phones!

BLOCKING WIRES AND T-PINS are essential for revealing the full beauty of lace patterns, which have to be stretched while wet to fully open the holes created by the yarnovers.

Although you can block your projects on the floor or a spare bed, BLOCKING MATS are good investments. Modular foam mats and boards made specifically for knitting are available at most yarn shops. Most are marked with grid lines that are helpful when blocking to certain measurements. You can purchase similar foam mats that are typically larger and without grids (but cheaper) at home improvement stores. Blocking mats are an advantage because once the knitting is pinned in place, the mat can be moved to another room or even stand upright against a wall.

charts

When it comes to knitting lace patterns, the power of charts is unquestionable. Charts graphically present the stitch manipulations in such a way that the symbols on the chart mimic the appearance of the right side of the completed knitting.

Once you understand how the symbols relate to the knitted stitches, you'll find that charts are easier to follow than row-by-row instructions and that errors are easier to detect. For example, yarnovers, which form intentional holes in the fabric, are represented by open circles on the chart. Decreases, which cause the stitches to lean to the left or right in the knitting, are represented by left- or right-leaning slanted lines on the chart. Although most of the symbols are intuitive once you're familiar with them, every chart is accompanied by a key that defines how to work the stitch represented by each symbol.

In general, each cell on a chart represents one stitch. Charts are read from bottom to top and from right to left for right-side rows and from left to right for wrong-side rows. Typically, odd-numbered rows are right-side rows and are numbered along the right edge of the chart, indicating that these rows are

Millersville

							10
			O	⅄	O		8
	O	∕			∖	O	6
	O	⅄	O	∕		O	
∖	O					O	∕	4
	∖	O		O	∕		2

7-st repeat

☐ knit on RS rows and all rnds; purl on WS rows

• purl on RS rows and all rnds; knit on WS rows

O yo

∕ k2tog on RS rows and all rnds; p2tog on WS rows

∖ ssk on RS rows and all rnds; p2tog tbl on WS rows

⅄ sl 1, k2tog, psso

☐ pattern repeat

A chart is a visual representation of the completed knitting.

worked from right to left. Wrong-side rows are often not labeled—you need to remember that they're worked from left to right. It's important to note that some chart symbols represent stitches that are worked differently on right- and wrong-side rows. For example, a purl stitch is denoted by a single dot when viewed from the right side, but the same appearance is achieved by knitting a stitch on a wrong-side row. Be sure to check the key for stitches that are worked differently on right- and wrong-side rows. For projects worked in rounds, every round is considered a right-side row, so every row of the chart is read from right to left.

Many new lace knitters struggle with reading the repeat boxes on charts. These boxes, typically outlined in red, are used to condense a chart into the smallest possible representation of the fabric. If the repeat box extends across the entire width of the chart, simply work from edge to edge (from right to left for right-side rows and from left to right for wrong-side rows) the necessary number of times to the end of the stitches on your needles. If the repeat box sits in the center of the chart, work the stitches to the right edge of the box (for right-side rows), then work the group of stitches within the box as many times as instructed or until the number of stitches remaining on your needles matches the number of stitches to the left of the repeat box, then work the stitches to the left of the repeat box.

Because a chart represents the knitting, you can compare your knitting to the chart to make sure you haven't made any mistakes. If yarnover symbols form diagonal lines in the chart, they should do the same in your knitting. If diagonal decrease lines come together in a point in the chart, the same should happen in your knitting. If your knitting doesn't look the same as the chart, you've likely made a mistake. In such cases, rip back to the place where your knitting matches the chart (this is where lifelines come in handy; see page 10), then proceed again.

If you're intimidated by the amount of information represented by a chart, narrow your view to focus on just the row at hand. Use a Post-it note, highlighter tape, or magnet board to hide the rows above the one you're currently working. This will help your eye focus on the chart row that coordinates to the row you're knitting and, by hiding what has yet to be worked, you'll only see the rows that have already been worked, which will correspond to the rows that have already been knitted.

lifelines

Lifelines are simply lengths of smooth contrasting thread that are drawn through an entire row of stitches that is known to have no mistakes. The lifelines don't affect the knitting, but they do allow you to rip back to a lifeline row without fear of dropping stitches, which can easily happen when yarn-overs are involved.

To insert a lifeline, thread a tapestry needle with a smooth yarn lighter in weight than the project yarn. Sewing thread or unwaxed dental floss both work well.

Examine the stitches on the needle to ensure that there are no mistakes. You may find it helpful to count the stitches in each pattern repeat. Draw the tapestry needle purlwise through every stitch on the needle, skipping any stitch markers you come to. Cut the lifeline thread, leaving a tail about 4" (10 cm) hanging at each end of the row. Work the next row in pattern, being careful not to catch the lifeline thread in the stitches, then continue in the pattern until you want to add another lifeline or until you make a mistake that requires ripping out the knitting.

If you find you've made a mistake and need to rip out, remove the working needle, then carefully pull the working yarn to ravel the knitting until you reach the lifeline. Following the path of the lifeline exactly, insert the needle purlwise (from right to left) through each stitch. Leave the lifeline in place in case it's needed again and resume knitting.

blocking

After you spend hours kitting a beautiful lace garment or accessory, you'll want to block it to stretch open the stitches to reveal their hidden beauty. To prepare a piece for blocking, begin by soaking it for fifteen to twenty minutes in a basin filled with warm water with a bit of wool wash. I like to use rinse-free soaps such as Soak or Euclan. You can substitute a mild shampoo, but keep in mind that doing so will require rinsing.

Drain the water from the basin and rinse, if necessary. To avoid felting, be sure that the rinse water is the same temperature as the water used for soaking. Gently squeeze out the water, then roll the piece in a towel or spin it in a salad spinner to extract as much excess water as possible. Take care not to twist or wring the knitted piece to ensure against unintentional felting or breaking delicate threads.

Pin key measurements first and then place additional pins in smaller and smaller sections.

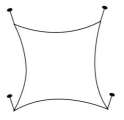 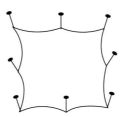 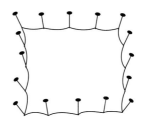

Using rustproof T-pins and blocking wires, carefully pin the damp piece to a clean flat surface, adjusting the pins and wires as necessary to achieve the desired shape and measurements. I recommend using a blocking mat, but carpet, towels, and non-water beds work just as well. If you're blocking a large piece, first pin the key points to measurements, then pin the smaller sections in between.

Be patient and wait for the piece to air-dry completely before removing the pins and wires. Depending on the temperature and the humidity, this will take about 24 hours.

Once thoroughly dried, remove the pins and wires, weave in the loose ends, and complete any required finishing.

Before blocking, the fabric has a wrinkled look, and lace patterns are difficult to see.

After blocking, the fabric opens up and smoothes to reveal the lace pattern.

CHAPTER 2

Warm

When I think of lace, images of light and airy fabrics often come to mind. Lace is perfect for the warm summer months. Tanks, shrugs, and other small accessories lend themselves beautifully to lace patterns. Knitted in lightweight yarns, the projects in this section are as delicate and flowing as soft summer breezes.

The **CHRISTIANA HEADBAND** (page 14) offers a chic alternative to rubber bands when the temperatures rise and you want to keep the hair off your face.

Sleeveless tops, such as the **MILLERSVILLE BLOUSE** (page 18), **PEQUEA SHELL** (page 26), and **EPHRATA CAMISOLE** (page 32), provide a bit of lace detail without adding extra warmth. Millersville features lace only on its flirty double layer edges; Pequea limits the lace to the back for dramatic effect; Ephrata showcases an allover lace pattern in a silky sumptuous yarn.

Both the **MANOR RIDGE SHRUG** (page 38) and **CONESTOGA TUNIC** (page 44) are ideal when just a light layer is in order. Place the Manor Ridge Shrug over your shoulders to take the chill out of an overly air-conditioned office. Knitted in a crisp linen yarn, the elegant Conestoga Tunic will take you from beach to boardwalk in lacy style.

Christiana
headband

The simple zigzag lace in this headband adorns the head with style. The ends of the lace section are folded in pleats where they join the button and buttonhole tabs. This project uses very little yarn; you can easily make one from sock yarn leftovers or make several from a full skein. They make great gifts for all the women in your life.

finished size
About 3½" (9 cm) wide and 18" (45.5 cm) head circumference, buttoned.

yarn
Fingering weight (#1 Super Fine).

Shown here: Baah! LaJolla (100% merino; 400 yd [366 m]/100 g): Raspberry Toffee, 1 skein (enough for 5 to 6 headbands).

needles
Size U.S. 4 (3.5 mm).

Adjust needle size if necessary to obtain the correct gauge.

notions
Tapestry needle; one ¾" (2 cm) button.

gauge
23 sts and 36 rows = 4" (10 cm) in zigzag lace patt.

NOTE

— Instead of working the button and buttonhole tabs at each end, you can work the lace section alone until it's long enough to be tied as a headscarf.

STITCH GUIDE

ZIGZAG LACE (even number of sts)

Set-up row: (WS) Sl 1, k2, purl to last 3 sts, k3.

Rows 1, 3, and 5: (RS) Sl 1, k2, *yo, k2tog; rep from * to last 3 sts, k3.

Even-numbered Rows 2–10: (WS) Sl 1, k2, purl to last 3 sts, k3.

Rows 7, 9, and 11: Sl 1, k2, *ssk, yo; rep from * to last 3 sts, k3.

Row 12: Rep Row 2.

Rep Rows 1–12 for patt; do not rep the set-up row.

RIBBING (odd number of sts)

Row 1: (WS) Sl 1, purl to end.

Row 2: (RS) Sl 1, *p1, k1; rep from *.

Rep Rows 1 and 2 for patt.

headband

CO 20 sts.

Work zigzag lace (see Stitch Guide) until piece measures 16½" (42 cm) from CO, ending with a WS row. BO all sts.

finishing

Block headband to about 3½" (9 cm) wide and 16½" (42 cm) long.

BUTTON TAB

Using the illustration on page 17 as a guide, fold one short end of the headband into pleats—pleated end measures about ¾" to 1" (2 to 2.5 cm) wide.

With RS facing, pick up and knit 7 sts across the pleated end, picking up through all layers of the folded pleats.

Work in ribbing patt (see Stitch Guide) until tab measures 2" (5 cm) from pick-up row when stretched.

BO all sts.

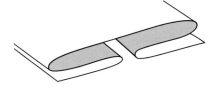

Fold short end into pleats.

BUTTONHOLE TAB

Fold the other short end into pleats according to illustration. With RS facing, pick up and knit 7 sts across the pleated end as for button tab. Work in ribbing patt until tab measures 1" (2.5 cm) from pick-up row when stretched, ending with a WS row.

BUTTONHOLE ROW: (RS) Work 2 sts in patt, work a 3-st one-row buttonhole (see Glossary), k2.

Cont in rib patt for ½" (1.3 cm) more.

BO all sts.

Sew button to button tab so that, when buttoned, the headband fits snuggly around the head.

Weave in loose ends.

Millersville
blouse

Knitted in the round from the bottom up, this flutter-sleeved top is as fun to wear as it is to knit. It features a square neckline and layered lace edges. A woven stitch on the straps provides stability for this luxuriously soft alpaca–cotton-blend yarn. Gathers at the sleeve caps and classic waist shaping add feminine touches.

finished size

About 32 (36, 40, 44, 48, 52)" (81.5 [91.5, 101.5, 112, 122, 132] cm) bust circumference. Sweater shown measures 32" (81.5 cm).

yarn

Sportweight (#2 Fine).

Shown here: Manos del Uruguay Serena (60% alpaca, 40% cotton; 170 yd [155 m]/50 g): #S2444 Harbor, 4 (5, 5, 6, 6, 7) skeins.

needles

Main body and sleeves: size U.S. 4 (3.5 mm): two 24" (60 cm) circular (cir).

Upper body and straps: size U.S. 6 (4 mm): straight.

Adjust needle size if necessary to obtain the correct gauge.

notions

Markers (m); stitch holders; tapestry needle.

gauge

28 sts and 36 rows/rnds = 4" (10 cm) in St st on smaller needles.

NOTES

- This top is knitted in the round from the bottom up to the armholes, then divided for working the front and back separately to the shoulders.
- The cap sleeves are worked back and forth, then sewn to the straps during finishing.

STITCH GUIDE

SHELL BORDER IN RNDS

(starts as multiple of 5 sts; ends as multiple of 4 sts)

Set-up row: (RS) *Yo, k5, pass 4 sts over the last knit st; rep from *–patt has dec'd to a multiple of 2 sts.

Place marker (pm) and join for working in the rnd with RS facing.

Rnd 1: *Work [k1, yo, k1tbl] all in same yo, k1; rep from *–patt has inc'd to a multiple of 4 sts.

Rnd 2: K1, *k1 tbl, k3; rep from * to last 3 sts, k1tbl, k2.

SHELL BORDER IN ROWS

(starts as multiple of 5 sts; ends as multiple of 4 sts)

Row 1: (RS) *Yo, k5, pass 4 sts over the last knit st; rep from * to end–patt has dec'd to a multiple of 2 sts.

Row 2: (WS) *P1, work [p1, yo, p1tbl] all in same yo; rep from * to end–patt has inc'd to a multiple of 4 sts.

Row 3: K1, *k1tbl, k3; rep from * to last 3 sts, k1tbl, k2.

WOVEN STITCH (even number of sts)

Row 1: (RS) Sl 1, *k1, sl 1 purlwise with yarn in front (pwise wyf); rep from * to last 3 sts, k3.

Rows 2 and 4: Sl 1, purl to end.

Row 3: Sl 1, k2, *sl 1 pwise wyf, k1; rep from * to last 3 sts, sl 1 pwise wyf, k2.

Rep Rows 1–4 for patt.

body border

note: *The border consists of two layers that will be laid one on top of the other and joined for working the body.*

BOTTOM LAYER

With the first smaller cir needle, CO 280 (315, 350, 385, 420, 455) sts. Do not join.

Working shell border in rnds (see Stitch Guide), work set-up row, then work Rnds 1 and 2 of patt— 224 (252, 280, 308, 336, 364) sts rem.

Purl 1 rnd, knit 1 rnd, purl 1 rnd— 2 garter ridges on RS.

Knit 13 rnds—piece measures about 2" (5 cm) from CO. Cut yarn and set aside, leaving sts on cir needle.

TOP LAYER

With the second smaller cir needle, CO 280 (315, 350, 385, 420, 455) sts. Do not join.

Working shell border in rnds, work set-up row, then work Rnds 1 and 2 of patt—224 (252, 280, 308, 336, 364) sts rem.

Work Rnds 1–11 of **MILLERSVILLE CHART**—piece measures about 1½" (3.8 cm) from CO. Do not cut yarn.

body

With RS of both layers facing, place top layer around the outside of the bottom layer, holding the needles parallel so that the bottom-layer needle is inside the circle of the top-layer needle.

JOINING RND: Using working yarn attached to top layer, *insert right needle tip of top layer needle into first st on top layer needle, then into first st

Millersville

7-st repeat

☐ knit on RS rows and all rnds; purl on WS rows

• purl on RS rows and all rnds; knit on WS rows

○ yo

╱ k2tog on RS rows and all rnds; p2tog on WS rows

╲ ssk on RS rows and all rnds; p2tog tbl on WS rows

⅄ sl 1, k2tog, psso

☐ pattern repeat

on bottom layer needle and k2tog (1 st from each needle); rep from * to end of rnd—224 (252, 280, 308, 336, 364) sts total on one needle.

NEXT RND: *Place marker (pm) for side, p1 for side "seam" st, k111 (125, 139, 153, 167, 181); rep from * once more.

Purling "seam" sts and slipping markers when you come to them, work rem sts even in St st until piece measures 1" (2.5 cm) from joining rnd and about 3" (7.5 cm) from bottom layer CO.

SHAPE WAIST

DEC RND: (RS) *P1, k2tog, knit to 2 sts before m, ssk, sl m; rep from * once more—4 sts dec'd.

[Work 13 rnds even in patt, then rep the dec rnd] 1 (2, 2, 2, 3, 3) time(s)—216 (240, 268, 296, 320, 348) sts rem.

[Work 11 rnds even, then rep the dec rnd] 3 (2, 2, 2, 1, 1) time(s)—204 (232, 260, 288, 316, 344) sts rem; piece measures 8¾ (9, 9, 9, 9, 9)" (22 [23, 23, 23, 23, 23] cm) from bottom layer CO.

Work even as established for 1" (2.5 cm).

INC RND: (RS) *P1, M1L (see Glossary), knit to m, M1R (see Glossary), sl m; rep from * once—4 sts inc'd.

[Work 11 rnds even, then rep the inc rnd] 3 (2, 2, 2, 1, 1) time(s), working new sts in St st—220 (244, 272, 300, 324, 352) sts.

[Work 13 rnds even, then rep the inc rnd] 1 (2, 2, 2, 3, 3) time(s)—224 (252, 280, 308, 336, 364) sts.

Work even as established for about ½" (1.3 cm) more, or until piece measures 16 (16½, 16½, 16½, 16½, 16½)" (40.5 [42, 42, 42, 42, 42] cm) from bottom layer CO.

divide for front and back

With RS facing, BO first 4 (5, 6, 7, 8, 9) sts of rnd, knit to next m, remove m, place last 112 (126, 140, 154, 168, 182) sts of rnd onto holder to work later for back, turn work.

front

With WS facing, BO 4 (5, 6, 7, 8, 9) sts, purl to end—104 (116, 128, 140, 152, 164) front sts rem.

SHAPE ARMHOLES

DEC ROW 1: (RS) Sl 1, sssk (see Glossary), ssk, knit to last 6 sts, k2tog, k3tog, k1—6 sts dec'd.

Work 1 WS row even.

Rep the last 2 rows 0 (0, 1, 2, 3, 4) more time(s)—98 (110, 116, 122, 128, 134) sts rem.

DEC ROW 2: (RS) Sl 1, sssk, knit to last 4 sts, k3tog, k1—4 sts dec'd.

Work 1 WS row even.

Rep the last 2 rows 0 (1, 2, 2, 3, 3) more time(s)—94 (102, 104, 110, 112, 118) sts rem.

SIZES (36, 40, 44, 48, 52)" ONLY

DEC ROW 3: (RS) Sl 1, ssk, knit to last 3 sts, k2tog, k1—2 sts dec'd.

Work 1 WS row even.

Rep the last 2 rows (1, 0, 1, 1, 2) more time(s)—(98, 102, 106, 108, 112) sts rem.

ALL SIZES

Change to larger needles. Work woven st (see Stitch Guide) on 94 (98, 102, 106, 108, 112) sts for 1½ (1½, 1¾, 1¾, 2, 2)" (3.8 [3.8, 4.5, 4.5, 5, 5] cm), ending with a WS row—armholes measure 2¼ (2¾, 3¼, 3¾, 4½, 5)" (5.5 [7, 8.5, 9.5, 11.5, 12.5] cm) from first armhole BO row.

SHAPE NECK

NEXT ROW: (RS) Work 12 (12, 14, 14, 14, 14) sts in patt and place these sts onto holder for left strap, BO center 70 (74, 74, 78, 80, 84) sts, work in patt to end—12 (12, 14, 14, 14, 14) right strap sts rem.

RIGHT STRAP

Work even in established patt until armhole measures 6½ (7¼, 7¾, 8¼, 8½, 9)" (16.5 [18.5, 19.5, 21, 21.5, 23] cm), ending with a WS row.

Cut yarn and place sts onto holder.

LEFT STRAP

Return 12 (12, 14, 14, 14, 14) held left strap sts to needle and rejoin yarn with WS facing. Work in established patt until armhole measures 6½ (7¼, 7¾, 8¼, 8½, 9)" (16.5 [18.5, 19.5, 21, 21.5, 23] cm), ending with a WS row.

Cut yarn and place sts onto holder.

back

Place 112 (126, 140, 154, 168, 182) held back sts onto smaller cir needle and rejoin yarn with RS facing. Working in St st, BO 4 (5, 6, 7, 8, 9) sts at beg of next 2 rows—104 (116, 128, 140, 152, 164) sts rem.

Shape armholes, neck, and straps as for front.

sleeve border

note: *The border consists of two layers that will be laid one on top of the other and joined for working the sleeve.*

BOTTOM LAYER

With the first smaller cir needle, CO 95 (95, 115, 130, 150, 160) sts. Do not join.

Work Rows 1–3 of shell border in rows (see Stitch Guide), beg and ending with a RS row—76 (76, 92, 104, 120, 128) sts rem.

Knit 3 rows, beg and ending with a WS row—2 garter ridges on RS.

Work even in St st for 12 rows, ending with a WS row.

Cont for your size as foll:

SIZES 32 (36, 44)" ONLY
NEXT ROW: (RS) K1, M1 (see Glossary), knit to end—77 (77, 105) sts.

SIZES (40, 48)" ONLY
NEXT ROW: (RS) K1, k2tog, knit to end—(91, 119) sts.

SIZES 52" ONLY
NEXT ROW: (RS) K1, [k2tog] 2 times, knit to end—126 sts.

ALL SIZES
77 (77, 91, 105, 119, 126) sts; piece measures about 2" (5 cm) from CO. Cut yarn and set aside, leaving sts on cir needle.

TOP LAYER
With the second smaller cir needle, CO 95 (95, 115, 130, 150, 160) sts. Do not join.

Work Rows 1–3 of shell border in rows, beg and ending with a RS row—76 (76, 92, 104, 120, 128) sts rem.

Work Row 1 of MILLERSVILLE CHART as a WS row for your size as foll:

SIZES 32 (36, 44)" ONLY
NEXT ROW: (WS) K1, M1, knit to end—77 (77, 105) sts.

SIZES (40, 48)" ONLY
NEXT ROW: (WS) K1, k2tog, knit to end—(91, 119) sts.

SIZES 52" ONLY
NEXT ROW: (WS) K1, [k2tog] 2 times, knit to end—126 sts.

ALL SIZES
Work Rows 2–11 of chart on 77 (77, 91, 105, 119, 126) sts; even-numbered chart rows are RS, and odd-numbered chart rows are WS—piece measures about 1½" (3.8 cm) from CO. Do not cut yarn.

sleeve
With RS of both layers facing and holding the needles parallel, place top layer on top of bottom layer.

JOINING ROW: (RS) Using working yarn attached to top layer, *insert right needle tip of top-layer needle into first st on top-layer needle, then into first st on bottom-layer needle and k2tog (1 st from each needle); rep from * to end—77 (77, 91, 105, 119, 126) sts total on one needle.

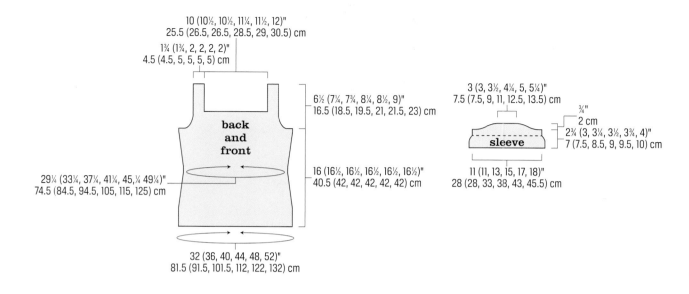

10 (10½, 10½, 11¼, 11½, 12)"
25.5 (26.5, 26.5, 28.5, 29, 30.5) cm

1¾ (1¾, 2, 2, 2, 2)"
4.5 (4.5, 5, 5, 5, 5) cm

6½ (7¼, 7¾, 8¼, 8½, 9)"
16.5 (18.5, 19.5, 21, 21.5, 23) cm

back and front

29¼ (33¼, 37¼, 41¼, 45,¼ 49¼)"
74.5 (84.5, 94.5, 105, 115, 125) cm

16 (16½, 16½, 16½, 16½, 16½)"
40.5 (42, 42, 42, 42, 42) cm

32 (36, 40, 44, 48, 52)"
81.5 (91.5, 101.5, 112, 122, 132) cm

3 (3, 3½, 4¼, 5, 5¼)"
7.5 (7.5, 9, 11, 12.5, 13.5) cm

¾"
2 cm

2¾ (3, 3¼, 3½, 3¾, 4)"
7 (7.5, 8.5, 9, 9.5, 10) cm

sleeve

11 (11, 13, 15, 17, 18)"
28 (28, 33, 38, 43, 45.5) cm

Work even in St st for ¾ (1, 1¼, 1½, 1¾, 2)" (2 [2.5, 3.2, 3.8, 4.5, 5] cm), ending with a WS row—piece measures 2¾ (3, 3¼, 3½, 3¾, 4)" (7 [7.5, 8.5, 9, 9.5, 10] cm) from bottom layer CO.

SHAPE CAP

BO 2 (2, 2, 3, 2, 3) sts at the beg of the next 2 rows, then BO 2 (2, 3, 3, 2, 3) sts at the beg of the foll 2 rows—69 (69, 81, 93, 111, 114) sts rem.

BO 3 sts at the beg of the next 2 rows—63 (63, 75, 87, 105, 108) sts rem.

NEXT ROW: (RS, gathering row) *Sl 1, k2tog, psso; rep from *—21 (21, 25, 29, 35, 36) sts rem.

BO all sts.

finishing

Place 12 (12, 14, 14, 14, 14) held right front strap sts on one needle and the corresponding held back strap sts on a second needle. Hold the needles parallel so that the RS of the straps are facing tog and the WS are facing out and use the three-needle method (see Glossary) to BO the sts tog. Rep to join the other shoulder.

Block to measurements.

Align the center of sleeve cap with the shoulder join. Working from the shoulder join down, use yarn threaded on a tapestry needle and the invisible vertical to horizontal seam (see Glossary) to sew the BO edge of the sleeve to the armhole edge of the strap, then continue sewing the St st selvedge of the lower sleeve to the armhole edge, ending at the 2 garter ridges above the chart patt, and leaving the sides of the sleeve borders unsewn.

note: *The cap is only large enough to fit the upper part of the armhole opening; the lower part of the armhole opening remains unfinished.*

Rep for other sleeve.

Weave in loose ends.

Pequea
shell

A lacy upper back gives sexy appeal to this silky camisole. It's worked in the round from the bottom up to the armholes, then the front and back pieces are worked back and forth in rows. At the top of the back, the piece divides into two straps that travel up and over the shoulder line and down the front to frame the neck opening. All edges are finished with a clean crochet border.

finished size

About 30¾ (34½, 38¼, 42, 45½)" (78 [87.5, 97, 106.5, 115.5] cm) bust circumference.

Tank shown measures 30¾" (78 cm).

yarn

Fingering weight (#1 Super Fine).

Shown here: Sweet Georgia Merino Silk Fine (50% merino, 50% silk; 380 yd [347 m]/100 g): Dutch, 2 (3, 3, 3, 3) skeins.

needles

Size U.S. 5 (3.75 mm): 24" (60 cm) circular (cir).

Adjust needle size if necessary to obtain the correct gauge.

notions

Markers (m); size F/5 (3.75 mm) crochet hook; tapestry needle.

gauge

28 sts and 36 rows/rnds = 4" (10 cm) in St st and lace patt from Pequea chart.

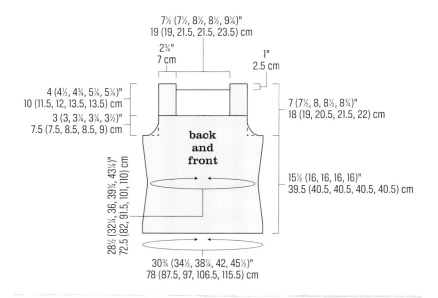

7½ (7½, 8½, 8½, 9¼)"
19 (19, 21.5, 21.5, 23.5) cm

2¾"
7 cm

1"
2.5 cm

4 (4½, 4¾, 5¼, 5¼)"
10 (11.5, 12, 13.5, 13.5) cm

3 (3, 3¼, 3¼, 3½)"
7.5 (7.5, 8.5, 8.5, 9) cm

7 (7½, 8, 8½, 8¾)"
18 (19, 20.5, 21.5, 22) cm

back and front

15½ (16, 16, 16, 16)"
39.5 (40.5, 40.5, 40.5, 40.5) cm

28½ (32¼, 36, 39¾, 43¼)"
72.5 (82, 91.5, 101, 110) cm

30¾ (34½, 38¼, 42, 45½)"
78 (87.5, 97, 106.5, 115.5) cm

body

CO 216 (242, 268, 294, 318) sts. Place marker (pm) and join for working in rnds, being careful not to twist sts. Rnd begins at left side, at start of front sts.

SET-UP RND: *P1 for "seam" st, k107 (120, 133, 146, 158), pm; rep from * once more, omitting pm because end-of-rnd m is already in place—108 (121, 134, 147, 159) sts each for front and back.

Purling the two "seam" sts every rnd, work rem sts in St st until piece measures 1½" (3.8 cm) from CO.

SHAPE WAIST

DEC RND: *P1, k2tog, knit to 2 sts before m, ssk, slip marker (sl m); rep from *—4 sts dec'd.

[Work 17 (19, 19, 19, 19) rnds even, then rep the dec rnd] 3 (1, 1, 1, 1) time(s)—200 (234, 260, 286, 310) sts rem; 100 (117, 130, 143, 155) sts each for front and back.

SIZES (34½, 38¼, 42, 45½)" ONLY

[Work 17 rnds even, then rep the dec rnd] 2 times—(226, 252, 278, 302) sts rem; (113, 126, 139, 151) sts each for front and back.

ALL SIZES

Work even as established for 1" (2.5 cm)—piece measures 8¼ (8¾, 8¾, 8¾, 8¾)" (21 [22, 22, 22, 22] cm) from CO.

INC RND: *P1, M1L (see Glossary), knit to m, M1R (see Glossary); rep from *—4 sts inc'd.

SIZES (34½, 38¼, 42, 45½)" ONLY

[Work 17 rnds even, then rep the inc rnd] 2 times—(234, 260, 286, 310) sts.

ALL SIZES

[Work 17 (19, 19, 19, 19) rnds even, then rep the inc rnd] 3 (1, 1, 1, 1) time(s)—216 (242, 268, 294, 318) sts; 108 (121, 134, 147, 159) sts each for front and back.

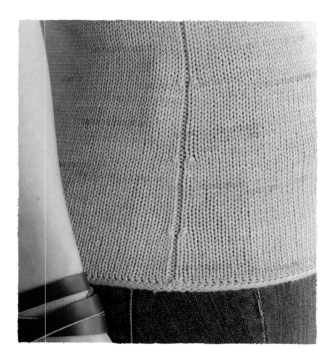

Pequea

\	O		O	⅄		O		O	/	7
	\	O		O	/	\	O		O	/	5
		O	⅄		O		O	⅄		O		3
O	/			\	O		O	/		\	O	1

6-st repeat

☐ knit on RS rows and all rnds;
  purl on WS rows

○ yo

/ k2tog

\ ssk

⅄ sl 1, k2tog, psso

☐ pattern repeat

Work even as established for 1"
(2.5 cm), ending last rnd 8 (15, 18, 25,
28) sts before end-of-rnd m—piece
measures about 15½ (16, 16, 16,
16)" (39.5 [40.5, 40.5, 40.5, 40.5] cm)
from CO.

DIVIDE FOR FRONT AND BACK

Removing markers as you come
to them, BO last 8 (15, 18, 25, 28)
back sts from end of previous rnd,
then BO first 5 (6, 7, 8, 9) front sts,
knit until there are 98 (110, 120, 131,
141) front sts on needle after BO gap,
BO last 5 (6, 7, 8, 9) front sts, then
the first 9 (14, 19, 25, 28) back sts—
98 (110, 120, 131, 141) front sts and
91 (91, 97, 97, 103) back sts rem.
Place front sts onto holder. Working
yarn is attached to start of back sts,
ready to work a RS row.

back

Working 91 (91, 97, 97, 103) back sts
back and forth in rows, purl 2 rows,
ending with a WS row—1 garter
ridge completed.

Beg with Rnd 1, work in pattt from
PEQUEA CHART until piece measures
6 (6½, 7, 7½, 7¾)" (15 [16.5, 18, 19,
19.5] cm) from start of lace section,
ending with a WS row.

SHAPE NECK

With RS facing, work 19 sts in patt,
BO center 53 (53, 59, 59, 65) sts,
work in patt to end—19 sts rem each
side.

Allow right strap sts to rest on the
needle while working the left strap.

LEFT STRAP

With WS facing and using working yarn attached to left strap sts, cont in established patt until strap measures 11 (12, 12¾, 13¾, 14)" (28 (30.5, 32.5, 35, 35.5] cm) from start of lace section and about 5 (5½, 5¾, 6¼, 6¼)" (12.5 [14, 14.5, 16, 16] cm) from back neck BO row, ending with a WS row.

Purl 2 rows, ending with a WS row—1 garter ridge completed.

Cut yarn and place sts onto holder.

RIGHT STRAP

With WS facing, rejoin yarn to 19 right strap sts and cont working in established patt until strap measures 11 (12, 12¾, 13¾, 14)" (28 (30.5, 32.5, 35, 35.5] cm) from start of lace section and about 5 (5½, 5¾, 6¼, 6¼)" (12.5 [14, 14.5, 16, 16] cm) from

back neck BO row, ending with a WS row.

Purl 2 rows, ending with a WS row—1 garter ridge completed.

Cut yarn and place sts onto holder.

front

Return 98 (110, 120, 131, 141) held front sts to needle and rejoin yarn with WS facing.

Work back and forth in rows as foll:

DEC ROW 1: (RS) Sl 1, [ssk] 2 times, knit to last 5 sts, [k2tog] 2 times, k1—4 sts dec'd.

NEXT ROW: (WS) Sl 1, purl to end.

Rep the last 2 rows 0 (1, 2, 4, 5) more time(s)—94 (102, 108, 111, 117) sts rem.

DEC ROW 2: Sl 1, ssk, knit to last 3 sts, k2tog, k1—2 sts dec'd.

NEXT ROW: Sl 1, purl to end.

Rep the last 2 rows 2 (4, 5, 6, 8) more times—88 (92, 96, 97, 99) sts rem.

Slipping the first st of every row as established, work rem sts in St st until armhole measures 3 (3, 3¼, 3¼, 3½)" (7.5 [7.5, 8.5, 8.5, 9] cm), ending with a WS row.

SHAPE NECK

NEXT ROW: (RS) Work 19 sts in patt, BO center 50 (54, 58, 59, 61) sts, work in patt to end—19 sts rem each side.

finishing

With yarn threaded on a tapestry needle, use the Kitchener st (see Glossary) to graft each set of 19 live front sts to corresponding set of 19 held strap sts.

EDGINGS

With crochet hook and RS facing, join yarn to CO edge of body at one side "seam." Work 1 rnd of single crochet (sc; see Glossary for crochet instructions), then work 1 rnd of back-post single crochet around lower edge. Break yarn and fasten off last st. Work edging in the same manner around each armhole opening, beg and ending in center of underarm.

Work edging in the same manner around neck opening, beg and ending at the right back neck corner.

Block to measurements. Weave in loose ends.

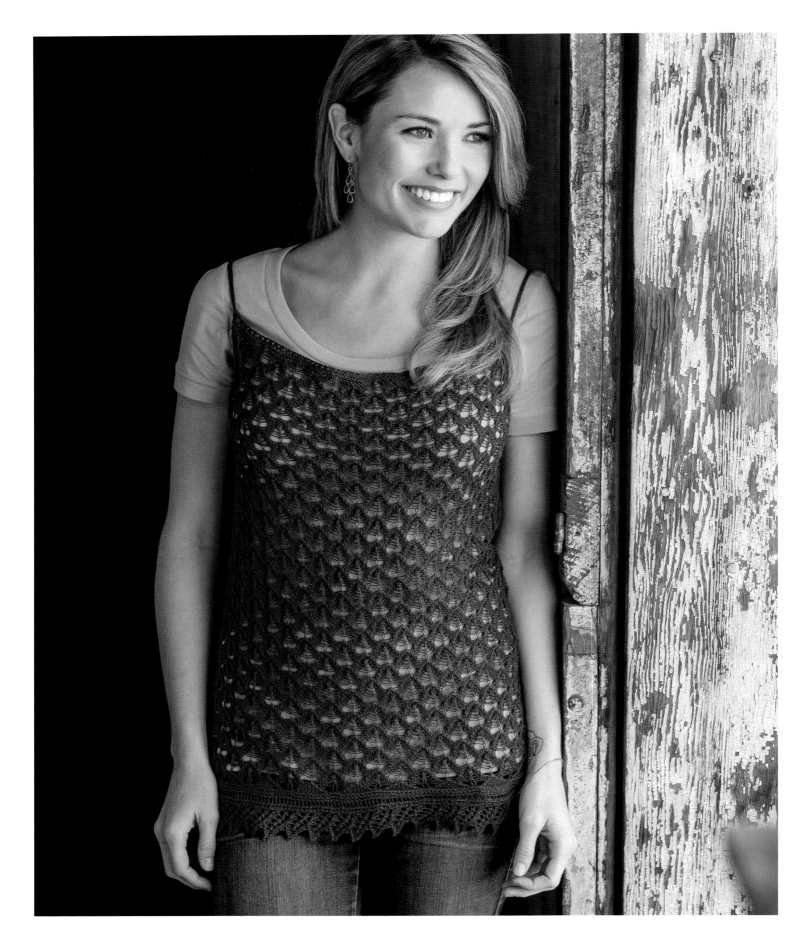

Ephrata
camisole

This delicate tank begins with a sideways-knitted sawtooth border from which the body stitches are picked up and worked in rounds. Although this project looks intimidating, the lack of waist shaping makes it quite straightforward, as there is no interruption to the lace pattern. The lace patterning on every row is less challenging on the lower body, which is worked in rounds. You'll have to pay more attention when working the upper body, which is worked back and forth in rows, but the beautiful results are worth the effort.

finished size
About 32 (35½, 39, 42½, 46, 49½)" (81.5 [90, 99, 108, 117, 125.5] cm) bust circumference.

Top shown measures 35½" (90 cm).

yarn
Laceweight (#0 Lace).

Shown here: Juniper Moon Farm Findley (50% merino, 50% silk; 798 yd [730 m]/100 g): #04 Renaissance, 1 (1, 2, 2, 2, 2) ball(s).

needles
Size U.S. 3 (3.25 mm): 24" (60 cm) circular (cir) and set of 2 double-pointed (dpn).

Adjust needle size if necessary to obtain the correct gauge.

notions
Markers (m); stitch holder; tapestry needle.

gauge
27½ sts and 40 rnds = 4" (10 cm) in patt from Ephrata Body chart, worked in rnds, blocked.

border

CO 10 sts.

Work Rows 1–10 of **EPHRATA BORDER CHART** 42 (47, 52, 56, 60, 65) times, then work Rows 1–9 once more.

NEXT ROW: (WS; counts as Row 10 of chart) Working in patt, BO until 1 st rem—43 (48, 53, 57, 61, 66) chart reps total.

With WS still facing, pick up and knit 214 (239, 264, 284, 304 329) sts along the straight selvedge of the border (end of WS rows; beg of RS rows), about 1 st from each of the 5 slipped selvedge sts in every 10-rnd patt rep—215 (240, 265, 285, 305, 330) sts total.

NEXT ROW: (RS) Knit, inc 5 (4, 3, 7, 11, 10) sts evenly spaced—220 (244, 268, 292, 316, 340) sts.

Place marker (pm) and join for working in rnds.

lower body and back

SET-UP RND: *P1 for side "seam" st, work Rnd 1 of **EPHRATA BODY CHART** over 109 (121, 133, 145, 157, 169) sts, pm for side seam; rep from * once more, omitting second pm because beg-of-rnd m is already in place.

Purling the "seam" sts every rnd, work rem sts in established patt until Rnds 1–10 of chart have been worked a total of 15 (15, 15, 15, 16, 16) times, then work Rnd 1 once more.

Ephrata Border

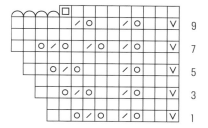

10 sts inc'd to 14 sts,
then dec'd to 10 sts again

Ephrata Body

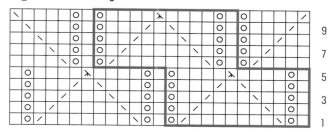

12-st repeat

GARTER EDGING FOR BACK AND ARMHOLES

note: *During the following section, if there are not enough stitches to work a single decrease with its companion yarnover, or a double decrease with both its companion yarnovers, work the remaining stitch(es) in stockinette.*

NEXT RND: (Rnd 2 of chart) Remove beg-of-rnd m, k9 (9, 11, 11, 12, 12), replace m for new beg-of-rnd, work in patt to 8 (8, 10, 10, 11, 11) sts before next m, pm for end of front sts, knit to side m, remove m, then knit to new beg-of-rnd m—93 (105, 113, 125, 135, 147) front sts at start of rnd; 127 (139, 155, 167, 181, 193) back and armhole sts at end of rnd.

RNDS 1 AND 3: Work front sts in established patt to m, sl m, purl to end of rnd.

RNDS 2 AND 4: Work front sts in established patt to m, sl m, knit to end of rnd.

RND 5: Rep Rnd 1 once more, ending 4 sts before end-of-rnd m—3 garter ridges for back and armholes.

NEXT RND: (Rnd 8 of chart) Sl 1 purlwise with yarn in back (wyb), k3, sl m, work front sts in patt to next m,

☐	knit on RS rows and all rnds; purl on WS rows
⊙	yo
╱	k2tog on RS rows and all rnds; p2tog on WS rows
╲	ssk on RS rows and all rnds; p2tog tbl on WS rows
⅄	sl 1, k2tog, psso on RS rows and all rnds; p3tog tbl on WS rows
⋁	sl 1 knitwise
⌒	BO 1 st
⊡	st on right needle after last BO
◼	pattern repeat

k4, loosely BO 119 (131, 147, 159, 173, 185) sts until 4 sts rem before beg-of-rnd m (1 st on right needle after final BO, and 3 sts on left needle before m)—101 (113, 121, 133, 143, 155) total sts rem; 93 (105, 113, 125, 135, 147) front sts in patt and 4 edging sts at each side; garter edging measures about ½" (1.3 cm) above last chart rnd on back.

front

note: *Change to working front sts back and forth in rows; see Glossary for sssk instructions.*

NEXT ROW: (RS; Row 9 of chart) K3 rem edging sts (now 4 sts on right needle), sl m, ssk (ssk, ssk, sssk, sssk,

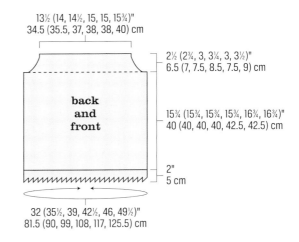

13½ (14, 14½, 15, 15, 15¾)"
34.5 (35.5, 37, 38, 38, 40) cm

2½ (2¾, 3, 3¼, 3, 3½)"
6.5 (7, 7.5, 8.5, 7.5, 9) cm

back and front

15¾ (15¾, 15¾, 15¾, 16¾, 16¾)"
40 (40, 40, 40, 42.5, 42.5) cm

2"
5 cm

32 (35½, 39, 42½, 46, 49½)"
81.5 (90, 99, 108, 117, 125.5) cm

k3tog), sl m, k4—2 (2, 2, 2, 4, 4) sts dec'd.

[Work 5 (1, 1, 1, 1, 1) row(s) even, then rep Dec Row 1] 1 (2, 7, 6, 7, 6) more time(s)—95 (105, 103, 115, 107, 123) sts rem.

Work 7 (3, 3, 1, 3, 1) row(s) even in patt.

DEC ROW 2: (RS) Sl 1 purlwise, k3, sl m, ssk, work in patt to 2 sts before m, k2tog, sl m, k4—2 sts dec'd.

SIZES (35½, 39, 42½, 46, 49½)" ONLY

[Work (3, 3, 1, 3, 1) row(s) even, then rep Dec Row 2] (3, 1, 5, 1, 6) more time(s), ending with a RS row— (97, 99, 103, 103, 109) sts rem.

ALL SIZES

Cont on 93 (97, 99, 103, 103, 109) sts, knit 5 rows beg and ending with a WS row—3 garter ridges when viewed from RS.

Next row: (RS) K4 for left strap and place these sts onto holder, BO 85 (89, 91, 95, 95, 101) center front sts, knit to end for right strap—4 right strap sts rem on needle.

sssk), work in patt to 2 (2, 2, 3, 3, 3) sts before m, k2tog (k2tog, k2tog, k3tog, k3tog, k3tog), sl m, k4—99 (111, 119, 129, 139, 151) sts rem.

Working the first 4 sts of every row as sl 1 knitwise, p3, and working the last 4 sts of every row as k4, work 5 (1, 1, 1, 1, 1) row(s) even in established patt, ending with a WS row.

DEC ROW 1: (RS) Sl 1 purlwise, k3, sl m, ssk (ssk, ssk, ssk, sssk, sssk), work in patt to 2 (2, 2, 2, 3, 3) sts before m, k2tog (k2tog, k2tog, k2tog, k3tog,

STRAPS

Transfer right strap sts to dpn and work in 4-st I-cord (see Glossary) until strap measures about 10 (10¾, 11½, 12¼, 12½, 13)" (25.5 [27.5, 29, 31, 31.5, 33] cm) from last row of front. Place strap sts onto holder or safety pin, and cut yarn, leaving a 1-yd (1-meter) tail for making adjustments. Return 4 held left strap sts to dpn, and work as for right strap.

note: *Although the upper back is bound off straight across as shown by the dotted line on the schematic, when the garment is worn, the straps will draw the upper edge of the back up into two points about 1½" (3.8 cm) high, which will contribute to the overall armhole height. The strap lengths given above will produce armhole heights of about 7 (7½, 8, 8½, 8½, 9)" (18 [19, 20.5, 21.5, 21.5, 23] cm) when worn.*

finishing

With yarn threaded on a tapestry needle, sew BO and CO ends of border tog at lower side of body. Block to measurements.

Temporarily pin the ends of the straps to the BO edge of upper back about 2" (5 cm) in from the purled "seam" st at each side. Try on the camisole, then adjust the placement of the straps, if necessary, by adding or removing I-cord rows to achieve the desired fit, then BO all sts for each strap leaving a 10" (25.5 cm) tail. Use tails threaded on a tapestry needle to sew the straps to the BO edge of upper back.

Weave in loose ends.

Manor Ridge
shrug

This little shrug is the perfect accessory to dress up a simple camisole or a little sundress. It adds just a touch of warmth across the back and shoulders and looks so pretty! Knitted from the top down, this shrug features mock-cable raglan details and is completely seamless. Stitches are picked up around the body and sleeve openings for the simple ribbed edgings, which are worked in the round.

finished size
About 29 (33½, 39, 42½, 46, 50)" (73.5 [85, 99, 108, 117, 127] cm) bust circumference.
Shrug shown measures 33½" (85 cm).

yarn
Fingering weight (#1 Super Fine).
Shown here: Regia Silk 4-ply (55% merino, 25% nylon, 20% silk; 218 yd [199 m]/50 g): #05 Linen, 2 (2, 2, 2, 3, 3) skeins.

needles
Size U.S. 3 (3.25 mm): 24" (60 cm) circular (cir) and set of 4 or 5 double-pointed (dpn).
Adjust needle size if necessary to obtain the correct gauge.

notions
Markers (m); stitch holder; tapestry needle.

gauge
29 sts and 42 rows = 4" (10 cm) in lace patt from Manor Ridge Body chart.

NOTES

— The body and raglan charts repeat over a different number of rows; keep track of each chart separately.

— For each 7-stitch raglan panel, repeat Rows 1–4 of the **MANOR RIDGE RAGLAN CHART** for the pattern.

— For the **MANOR RIDGE BODY CHART,** the first time you work through the chart there will be enough stitches in Rows 1–14 to work the 8-stitch red outlined pattern repeat 3 (4, 6, 6, 7, 8) times across the back and once for each sleeve. In Rows 15–34, enough stitches will have been increased to work the 8-stitch pattern repeat 5 (6, 8, 8, 9, 10) times across the back and 3 times for each sleeve. In Rows 35–48, enough stitches will have been increased to work the 8-stitch pattern repeat 7 (8, 10, 10, 11, 12) times across the back and 5 times for each sleeve. Continue in this manner when the chart begins over again at Row 1, working the 8-stitch repeat as many times as necessary to accommodate the number of stitches.

STITCH GUIDE

MOCK CABLE (worked over 3 sts)

Use the right needle tip to lift the third st on left needle over the first and second sts and off the needle, then work the first and second sts on left needle as k1, yo, k1—3 sts made from 3 sts.

yoke

With cir needle, CO 1 st for left front, place marker (pm), CO 7 sts for left front raglan, pm, CO 11 sts for left sleeve, pm, CO 7 sts for left back raglan, pm, CO 27 (35, 51, 51, 59, 67) back sts, pm, CO 7 sts for right back raglan, pm, CO 11 sts for right sleeve, pm, CO 7 sts for right front raglan, pm, CO 1 st for right front—79 (87, 103, 103, 111, 119) sts total.

NEXT ROW: (WS) Purl.

☐	knit on RS rows; purl on WS rows
⊙	yo
╱	k2tog on RS rows; p2tog on WS rows
╲	ssk on RS rows; p2tog tbl on WS rows
⋊	sl 1, k2tog, psso
☐	no stitch
☐	pattern repeat
—⊙—	mock cable (see Stitch Guide)

Manor Ridge Body

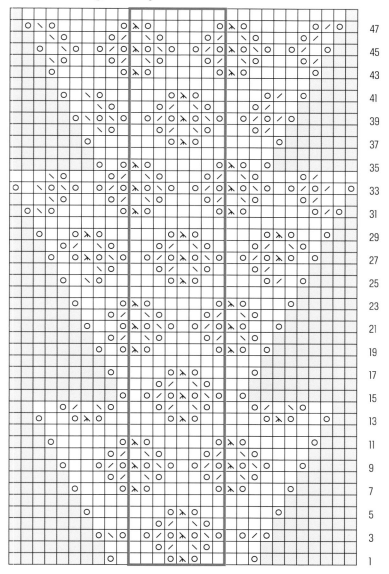

8-st repeat
See Notes.

Manor Ridge Raglan

7-st panel

NEXT ROW: (RS) Sl 1 left front st, slip marker (sl m), work **RAGLAN CHART** over 7 sts, sl m, work **BODY CHART** over 11 left sleeve sts inc 2 sts as shown, sl m, work **RAGLAN CHART** over 7 sts, sl m, work **BODY CHART** over back sts inc 2 sts as shown, sl m, work **RAGLAN CHART** over 7 sts, sl m, work **BODY CHART** over 11 right sleeve sts inc 2 sts as shown, sl m, work **RAGLAN CHART** over 7 sts, sl m, k1 right front st—6 sts inc'd; 2 sts each sleeve and 2 back sts.

NEXT ROW: (WS) Sl 1 right front st, work in established patts to last st, p1 left front st.

Working the first and last st of each row as established in the previous 2 rows, cont in patt for 58 (64, 70, 74, 76, 82) more rows (see Notes), ending with Row 12 (18, 24, 28, 30, 36) of **BODY CHART** and Row 4 (2, 4, 4, 2, 4) of **RAGLAN CHART**—259 (285, 319, 331, 345, 371) sts total; 1 st each front, four 7-st raglan sections, 71 (77, 83, 87, 89, 95) sts each sleeve, 87 (101, 123, 127, 137, 151) back sts; piece measures 5¾ (6½, 7, 7¼, 7½, 8)" (14.5 [16.5, 18, 18.5, 19, 20.5] cm) from CO measured straight up at center back.

DIVIDING ROW: (RS) Removing markers when you come to them and cont in patt, sl 1 front st, work 7 raglan sts, place next 71 (77, 83, 87, 89, 95) left sleeve sts onto holder, use the backward-loop method (see Glossary) to CO 3 (5, 3, 11, 13, 15) sts for left underarm, work 7 raglan sts, work 87 (101, 123, 127, 137, 151) back sts inc 2 sts as shown on chart, work 7 raglan sts, place next 71 (77, 83, 87, 89, 95) right sleeve sts onto holder, use the backward-loop method to CO 3 (5, 3, 11, 13, 15) sts for right underarm, work 7 raglan sts, k1— 125 (143, 161, 181, 195, 213) sts rem.

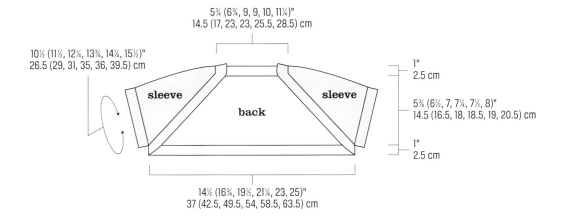

5¾ (6¾, 9, 9, 10, 11¼)"
14.5 (17, 23, 23, 25.5, 28.5) cm

10½ (11½, 12¼, 13¾, 14¼, 15½)"
26.5 (29, 31, 35, 36, 39.5) cm

sleeve

back

sleeve

1"
2.5 cm

5¾ (6½, 7, 7¼, 7½, 8)"
14.5 (16.5, 18, 18.5, 19, 20.5) cm

1"
2.5 cm

14½ (16¾, 19½, 21¼, 23, 25)"
37 (42.5, 49.5, 54, 58.5, 63.5) cm

body edging

With RS still facing, pick up and knit 31 (34, 37, 39, 40, 43) sts along right front from end of live body sts to CO edge, 77 (85, 101, 101, 109, 117) sts across CO between front sts, and 31 (34, 37, 39, 40, 43) sts along left front from CO to live body sts—264 (296, 336, 360, 384, 416) sts total. Pm and join for working in rnds.

NEXT RND: *K2, p2; rep from *.

Rep the last rnd until ribbed edging measures 1" (2.5 cm) from pick-up rnd.

Loosely BO all sts in patt.

sleeve edging

Arrange 71 (77, 83, 87, 89, 95) held sleeve sts as evenly as possible on 3 or 4 dpn. With RS facing, join yarn at start of underarm CO sts, pick up and knit 5 (7, 5, 13, 15, 17) sts evenly spaced along sts CO at underarm, pm, and join for working in rnds—76 (84, 88, 100, 104, 112) sts total.

Work in k2, p2 ribbing as for body edging for 1" (2.5 cm).

Loosely BO all sts in patt.

finishing

Block to measurements. Weave in loose ends.

Conestoga tunic

Worked from the bottom up, this loose-fitting cover-up features minimal shaping and button closures. The T-shaped front and back pieces are worked separately, then seamed together. Wear the tunic over a swimsuit or camisole for just a little extra coverage. Crisp linen yarn keeps you cool and carefree whether at the beach or in the mall.

finished size
About 39 (43, 47½, 51½, 56, 60)" (99 [109, 120.5, 131, 142, 152.5] cm) bust circumference, intended to be worn with a generous amount of positive ease.

Sweater shown measures 39" (99 cm).

yarn
Fingering weight (#1 Super Fine).

Shown here: Quince and Company Sparrow (100% organic linen; 168 yd [154 m]/50 g): #202 Birch, 7 (8, 9, 10, 10, 11) skeins.

needles
Size U.S. 5 (3.75 mm).

Adjust needle size if necessary to obtain the correct gauge.

notions
Tapestry needle; six ½" (1.3 cm) buttons.

gauge
23 sts and 30 rows = 4" (10 cm) in lace patt from Conestoga chart; 3-st garter edges at each side of body measure ⅜" (1 cm) wide.

back

LOWER BODY

CO 114 (126, 138, 150, 162, 174) sts.

Knit 6 rows, ending with a WS row—3 garter ridges completed; piece measures about ½" (1.3 cm).

SET-UP ROW: (RS) K3, work Row 1 of **CONESTOGA CHART** over center 108 (120, 132, 144, 156, 168) sts, k3.

Keeping 3 sts at each side in garter st (knit every row), work rem sts in chart patt until Rows 1–8 of chart have been worked a total of 15 (16, 16, 16, 16, 16) times; do not turn at end of last WS row—120 (128, 128, 128, 128, 128) chart rows completed; piece measures about 16½ (17½, 17½, 17½, 17½, 17½)" (42 [44.5, 44.5, 44.5, 44.5, 44.5] cm) from CO.

SLEEVES

With WS still facing, use the backward-loop method (see Glossary) to CO 48 sts at end of needle—162 (174, 186, 198, 210, 222) sts total.

NEXT ROW: (RS) K3, work Row 1 of chart over 156 (168, 180, 192, 204, 216) sts, k3, then use the backward-loop method to CO 48 sts at end of needle—210 (222, 234, 246, 258, 270) sts total.

NEXT ROW: (WS) K3, work Row 2 of chart over center 204 (216, 228, 240, 252, 264) sts, k3.

Keeping 3 sts at each side in garter st, work rem sts in chart patt until Rows 1–8 of chart have been worked 8 (8, 8, 9, 9, 10) times from beg of sleeve—piece measures about 8½ (8½, 8½, 9½, 9½, 10¾)" (21.5 [21.5, 21.5, 24, 24, 27.5] cm) from sleeve CO.

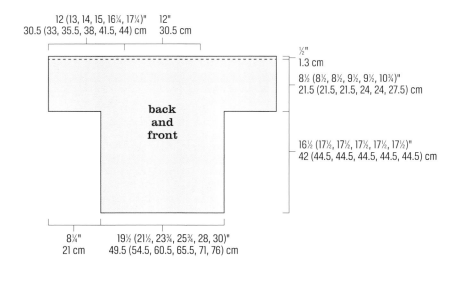

12 (13, 14, 15, 16¼, 17¼)"
30.5 (33, 35.5, 38, 41.5, 44) cm   12"
                                   30.5 cm

½"
1.3 cm

8½ (8½, 8½, 9½, 9½, 10¾)"
21.5 (21.5, 21.5, 24, 24, 27.5) cm

back and front

16½ (17½, 17½, 17½, 17½, 17½)"
42 (44.5, 44.5, 44.5, 44.5, 44.5) cm

8¼"
21 cm   19½ (21½, 23¾, 25¾, 28, 30)"
        49.5 (54.5, 60.5, 65.5, 71, 76) cm

Conestoga

12-st repeat

□	knit on RS rows; purl on WS rows
•	purl on RS rows; knit on WS rows
○	yo
╱	k2tog on RS rows; p2tog on WS rows
╲	ssk on RS rows; p2tog tbl on WS rows
⼂	k3tog on RS rows; p3tog on WS rows
⼃	sssk on RS rows; p3tog tbl on WS rows
■	pattern repeat

BUTTONBAND

Knit 6 rows, working [k1, p1] in each double yo of the lace patt in the first row—band measures ½" (1.3 cm) above last patt row.

Loosely BO all sts.

Mark center of BO edge. Mark placement of two buttons, each 6" (15 cm) out from the center to mark a 12" (30.5 cm) boatneck opening, or wherever desired neck width is achieved. Mark placement of rem two buttons ½" (1.3 cm) in from each end of BO row.

front

CO and work as for back to buttonband—210 (222, 234, 246, 258, 270) sts; piece measures about 8½ (8½, 8½, 9½, 9½, 10¾)" (21.5 [21.5, 21.5, 24, 24, 27.5] cm) from sleeve CO.

BUTTONHOLE BAND

Knit 2 rows, working [k1, p1] in each double yo of the lace patt on the first row and ending with a WS row.

Mark placement of four buttonholes to correspond to button markers on buttonband.

BUTTONHOLE ROW: (RS) Knit, working [yo, k2tog] at each buttonhole position.

Knit 3 more rows—band measures ½" (1.3 cm) from last patt row.

Loosely BO all sts.

finishing

Block to measurements. Weave in loose ends.

With yarn threaded on a tapestry needle, sew lower sleeve and side seams, beg at lower edge of sleeve opening and ending 3" (7.5 cm) above body CO edge, leaving lower 3" (7.5 cm) of side seams open for side slits. Upper edge remains unsewn.

Sew four buttons to buttonband, opposite buttonholes. Sew one decorative button at the top of each side slit, at the base of each side seam.

CHAPTER 3

Transitional

Spring and fall are my favorite seasons. The temperatures verge on chilly, and the colors of nature are vibrant. These are the times for light sweaters, garments that can be layered, and stylish accessories. You can wear the projects in this chapter anytime, anywhere.

Both the NARVON WRAP (page 50) and KIRKWOOD VEST (page 56) can be worn as light jackets or decorative wraps. Knitted with silk-and-wool-blend yarns, they provide a delicate lacy layer of light warmth. The TERRE HILL TUNIC (page 60), knitted with crisp linen yarn, can be worn on its own when days are warm or over other layers when the weather turns brisk.

Socks and arm warmers are welcome accessories during cool spring rains, blustery fall gusts, or anytime there's a chill. The SWATARA (page 66) and MILLWAY (page 74) socks will keep your toes toasty on autumn walks and in drafty houses. The STRASBURG ARM WARMERS (page 80) can provide an extra layer on your arms—make them long or short for the desired amount of coverage.

Narvon
wrap

This circular vest begins in the center with a leaf motif that radiates outward then transitions to reversible textured lace. Simple garter stitch around the armholes and outer edge keep the focus on the intricate lace medallion. The wrap can be worn secured in front with a shawl pin, or it can be left open so the outer rings of the circle drape beautifully.

finished size

About 35½ (39, 42½, 46, 49½, 53)" (90 [99, 108, 117, 125.5, 134.5]cm) in diameter and 15¼ (15¾, 16¼, 16¾, 17¼, 17¾)" (38.5 [40, 41.5, 42.5, 44. 45]cm) back width between base of armhole openings.

Vest shown measures 35½" in diameter.

yarn

Sportweight (#2 Fine).

Shown here: Madelinetosh Pashmina (75% merino, 15% silk, 10% cashmere; 360 yd [329 m]/115 g): Isadora, 4 (5, 5, 6, 7, 8) skeins.

needles

Size U.S. 5 (3.75 mm): 24" (60 cm) and 32" (80 cm) circular (cir) and set of 4 or 5 double-pointed (dpn).

Adjust needle size if necessary to obtain the correct gauge.

notions

Markers (m); waste yarn; tapestry needle.

gauge

26 sts and 32 rnds = 4" (10 cm) in textured patt from Narvon Chart C, worked in rnds.

NOTES

— In order to keep the pattern properly aligned, it will be necessary to "borrow" one stitch from the end of the previous round to work the double decrease at the start of Rnd 36 (shaded in blue on the chart). Prepare for the "loan" by knitting Rnd 35 to the last stitch, temporarily slip the last stitch (shaded in blue) to the right needle, remove the marker, return the slipped stitch to the left needle, and replace the marker. Work the blue-shaded double decrease at the start of the Rnd 36 using the "borrowed" stitch with the following two stitches.

— Convert this vest into a cardigan by working the picked-up stitches from the armhole edgings as sleeves.

— Wear the vest upside down, with the longer body portion at the top, for a deeper collar and shorter body.

Narvon Chart A

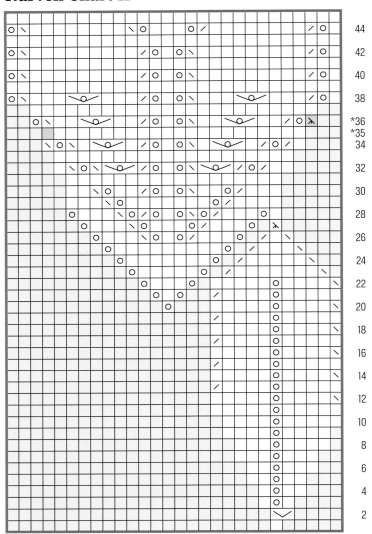

1-st repeat inc'd to 28-st repeat
*See Notes.

☐ knit	⋌ sl 1, k2tog, psso
• purl	☐ no stitch
○ yo	▨ see Notes
⁄ k2tog	▣ pattern repeat
⟍ ssk	⌄ k1f&b
⟋ p2tog	⌄○ work [k1, yo, k1] in same st

Narvon Chart B

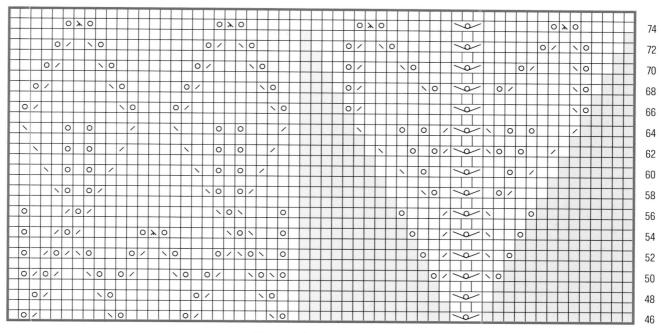

74
72
70
68
66
64
62
60
58
56
54
52
50
48
46

28-st repeat inc'd to 58-st repeat

back

Using Emily Ocker's method (see Glossary), CO 8 sts. Divide sts evenly onto 4 dpn so that there are 2 sts on each needle.

Place marker (m) and join for working in rnds, being careful not to twist sts.

Work Rnds 1–45 of **NARVON CHART A**, inc as shown and changing to 24" (60 cm) cir needle when there are too many sts to fit around the dpn—224 sts.

Work Rnds 46–62 (64, 66, 68, 70, 72) of **NARVON CHART B**, inc as shown and changing to 32" (80 cm) cir needle when necessary—368 (384, 400, 416, 432, 448) sts; 46 (48, 50, 52, 54, 56) sts each in 8 patt reps; piece measures about 7¾ (8, 8, 8¼, 8½, 8¾) (19.5 [20.5, 20.5, 21, 21.5, 22] cm)" from CO.

MARK ARMHOLES

NEXT RND: (Rnd 63 [65, 67, 69, 71, 73] of chart) With waste yarn, k46 (49, 52, 55, 57, 60) to mark the right armhole, then return the waste-yarn sts just worked to the left needle tip. With working yarn, knit the waste yarn sts again, then knit the next 91 (94, 98, 99, 102 106) sts. With another piece of waste yarn, k46 (49, 52, 55, 57, 60) to mark the left armhole, then return the waste-yarn sts just worked to the left needle tip. With working yarn, knit the waste-yarn sts again, then knit 185 (192, 198, 207, 216, 222) sts to end of rnd.

Cont in patt until Rnd 75 of **NARVON CHART B** has been completed for all sizes—464 sts; 58 sts each in 8 patt reps; piece measures about 9¼" (23.5 cm) from CO.

Narvon Chart C

		13
		11
		9
		7
		5
		3
		1

2-st repeat,
inc'd to 4-st repeat,
then dec'd to 2-st repeat

☐ knit

• purl

○ yo

╱ k2tog

╲ ssk

⟍ p2tog

⅄ sl 1, k2tog, psso

☐ no stitch

▨ see Notes

☐ pattern repeat

⌄ k1f&b

⌣ work [k1, yo, k1] in same st

OUTER EDGING

[Purl 1 rnd, knit 1 rnd] 2 times, then purl 1 more rnd—3 garter ridges completed.

Work Rnds 1–14 of **NARVON CHART C**.

NEXT RND: (inc rnd) [K8, k1f&b (see Glossary)] 16 times, [k9, k1f&b] 32 times—512 sts.

Purl 1 rnd, knit 1 rnd, purl 1 rnd— 2 garter ridges completed.

Work Rnds 1–14 of **NARVON CHART C** 2 (3, 4, 5, 6, 7) times.

[Purl 1 rnd, knit 1 rnd] 2 times— 2 garter ridges completed.

Work Rnds 1–14 of **NARVON CHART C** once more.

[Purl 1 rnd, knit 1 rnd] 5 times— 5 garter ridges completed; piece measures about 8½ (10¼, 12, 13¾, 15½, 17¼)" (21.5 [26, 30.5, 35, 39.5, 44] cm) from end of **NARVON CHART B** and about 17¾ (19½, 21¼, 23, 24¾,

26½)" (45 [49.5, 54, 58.5, 63, 67.5] cm) from CO.

BO all sts very loosely so the circle will lie flat.

finishing

Block to measurements.

ARMHOLE EDGINGS

Carefully remove waste yarn from armholes and distribute 91 (97, 103, 109, 113, 119) exposed sts as evenly as possible on 3 or 4 dpn.

NEXT RND: Knit, picking up 1 extra st in each "corner" of the armhole slit to prevent gaps—93 (99, 105, 111, 115, 121) sts.

[Purl 1 rnd, knit 1 rnd] 2 times, then purl 1 more rnd—6 rnds and 3 garter ridges completed.

Loosely BO all sts.

Weave in loose ends.

Kirkwood
vest

Shaped as a rectangle with armholes, this vest is both fun and easy to knit. It's worked from side to side in a luxurious silk-blend yarn that provides plenty of elegant drape. To minimize the interruption of the lace pattern, the armholes are marked with waste yarn, the same as afterthought sock heels, then the waste yarn is removed to expose live stitches for the armbands. The edges are finished with a few simple rows of garter stitch. As a bonus, this vest is completely reversible.

finished size

To fit bust circumferences of about 33½ (36, 37½, 41¾, 43¼, 45¼)" (85 [91.5, 95, 106, 110, 115] cm), with fronts overlapped about 4" (10 cm); fit is adjustable by increasing or decreasing the amount of overlap.

Vest shown is for 33½" (85 cm) bust circumference.

yarn

DK weight (#3 Light).

Shown here: Malabrigo Silky Merino (51% silk, 49% merino wool; 150 yd [137 m]/50 g): #412 Teal Feather, 6 (6, 7, 8, 8, 8) skeins.

needles

Size U.S. 7 (4.5 mm): 24" (60 cm) circular (cir) and set of 4 or 5 double-pointed (dpn).

Adjust needle size if necessary to obtain the correct gauge.

notions

Markers (m); a few yards of waste yarn to mark armhole openings; tapestry needle.

gauge

22½ sts and 30½ rows = 4" (10 cm) in lace patt from Kirkwood chart; 8-st garter edgings measure about 1½" (3.8 cm) wide.

NOTES

— The body is worked from side to side in one piece, beginning at the left front edge and ending at the right front edge.

— For neat edges, slip the first stitch of every row purlwise with yarn in front (wyf).

Kirkwood

5

3

1

4-st repeat,
dec'd to 2-st repeat,
then inc'd to 4-st repeat again

	knit on RS rows; purl on WS rows
·	purl on RS rows; knit on WS rows
⊙	yo
⊿	p4tog on RS rows and WS rows
	no stitch
▢	pattern repeat
⌵	work [k1, p1, k1] in yo on RS rows and WS rows

body

LEFT FRONT

With cir needle, CO 156 (164, 168, 172, 172, 176) sts. Work in garter st (knit every row) for 12 rows, ending with a WS row—6 garter ridges on RS; piece measures about 1½" (3.8 cm).

NEXT ROW: (RS) Sl 1 (see Notes), work 7 sts in garter st, place marker (pm), work Row 1 of **KIRKWOOD CHART** over center 140 (148, 152, 156, 156, 160) sts, pm, work 8 sts in garter st.

Working the first 8 sts as sl 1, k7 and the last 8 sts as k8 every row, work rem sts in chart patt until Rows 1–6 of patt have been worked 13 (14, 15, 17, 18, 19) times, then work Rows 1–5 once more, ending with a RS row.

MARK LEFT ARMHOLE

NEXT ROW: (WS; Row 6 of chart) Work 25 sts in patt, k35 (39, 41, 44, 45, 48) with waste yarn, return these 35 (39, 41, 44, 45, 48) sts to left needle, pick up working yarn and work across them in patt, then cont in patt to end of row—left front measures about 12½ (13¼, 14, 15¾, 16½, 17¼)" (31.5 [33.5, 35.5, 40, 42, 44] cm) from CO.

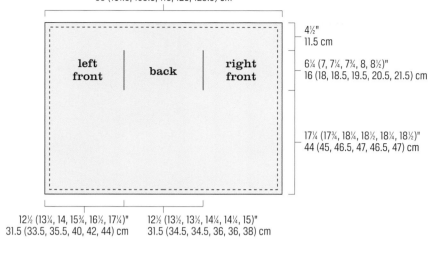

37½ (40, 41½, 45¾, 47¼, 49½)"
95 (101.5, 105.5, 116, 120, 125.5) cm

left
front

back

right
front

4½"
11.5 cm

6¼ (7, 7¼, 7¾, 8, 8½)"
16 (18, 18.5, 19.5, 20.5, 21.5) cm

17¼ (17¾, 18¼, 18½, 18¼, 18½)"
44 (45, 46.5, 47, 46.5, 47) cm

12½ (13¼, 14, 15¾, 16½, 17¼)"
31.5 (33.5, 35.5, 40, 42, 44) cm

12½ (13½, 13½, 14¼, 14¼, 15)"
31.5 (34.5, 34.5, 36, 36, 38) cm

BACK

Cont as established, work Rows 1–6 of **KIRKWOOD CHART** 15 (16, 16, 17, 17, 18) times, then work Rows 1–5 once more, ending with a RS row.

MARK RIGHT ARMHOLE

NEXT ROW: (WS; Row 6 of chart) Work 25 sts in patt, k35 (39, 41, 44, 45, 48) with waste yarn, return these 35 (39, 41, 44, 45, 48) sts to left needle, pick up working yarn and work across them in patt, then cont in patt to end of row—back measures 12½ (13½, 13½, 14¼, 14¼, 15)" (31.5 [34.5, 34.5, 36, 36, 38] cm) from left armhole waste-yarn row.

RIGHT FRONT

Cont as established, work Rows 1–6 of chart 14 (15, 16, 18, 19, 20) times, ending with a WS row. Work in garter for 12 rows, ending with a WS row—6 garter ridges on RS; right front measures about 12½ (13¼, 14, 15¾, 16½, 17¼)" (31.5 [33.5, 35.5, 40, 42, 44] cm) from right armhole

waste-yarn row; piece measures about 37½ (40, 41½, 45¾, 47¼, 49½)" (95 [101.5, 105.5, 116, 120, 125.5] cm) total from CO.

Loosely BO all sts.

finishing

Block to measurements.

ARMHOLE EDGINGS

With RS facing, carefully remove waste yarn from one armhole and divide 69 (77, 81, 87, 89, 95) exposed sts as evenly as possible on 3 or 4 dpn. Place marker (pm) and join for working in rnd.

SET-UP RND: Knit, picking up 1 extra st at the top and bottom of the armhole slit to prevent gaps—71 (79, 83, 89, 91, 97) sts.

[Purl 1 rnd, knit 1 rnd] 2 times, then purl 1 rnd—3 garter ridges.

Loosely BO all sts.

Terre Hill
tunic

This classy shell is worked from the bottom up in one piece to the armholes, then it divides and the back and front are worked separately to the shoulders.

It starts with a clean hem and ends with a garter-stitch neckline. The wide lace panel is flanked by ribbing that hugs the waist, creating a shaping effect. The crisp linen-blend yarn is light and sophisticated and offers great stitch definition.

finished size

About 29¾ (33¼, 37¼, 40¾, 44½, 48)" (75.5 [84.5, 94.5, 103.5, 113, 122] cm) bust circumference.
Tunic shown measures 33¼" (84.5 cm).

yarn

DK weight (#3 Light).

Shown here: Classic Elite Yarns Soft Linen (35% linen, 35% wool, 30% alpaca; 137 yd [125 m]/50 g): #2292 Lupine, 5 (6, 7, 7, 8, 9) balls.

needles

Size U.S. 5 (3.75 mm): 24" (60 cm) circular (cir).

Adjust needle size if necessary to obtain the correct gauge.

notions

Markers (m); stitch holders; tapestry needle.

gauge

26½ sts and 35 rows/rnds = 4" (10 cm) in St st and lace patt from Terre Hill chart; 13 Ribbing Panel sts measure 2" (5 cm) wide.

lower body

CO 196 (220, 246, 270, 294, 318) sts. Place marker (pm) and join for working in rnds, being careful not to twist sts.

Knit 6 rnds for hem facing, purl 1 rnd for fold line, knit 5 more rnds.

JOINING RND: Fold facing to WS along fold line; *insert right needle tip into first st on needle, then the CO st directly below it and k2tog (1 live st tog with 1 CO st); rep from *—still 196 (220, 246, 270, 294, 318) sts; hem measures about ¾" (2 cm) from fold line.

SET-UP RND: Work ribbing panel (see Stitch Guide) over 13 sts, k8 (14, 21, 24, 30, 36), p1, pm, work Rnd 1 of **TERRE HILL CHART** over 66 (66, 66, 73, 73, 73) center front st, pm, p1, k8 (14, 21, 23, 29, 35), work ribbing panel over 13 sts, knit to end—13 sts each in 2 ribbing panels, 84 (96, 110, 122, 134, 146) front sts, 86 (98, 110, 122, 134, 146) back sts.

Work in patts as established until piece measures 15¼ (16, 16, 16, 16¼, 16¼)" (38.5 [40.5, 40.5, 40.5, 41.5, 41.5] cm) from hem fold line, ending with an even-numbered chart rnd.

DIVIDE FRONT AND BACK

DIVIDING RND: (odd-numbered chart rnd) BO 13 sts of first ribbing panel, work in patt to next ribbing panel, BO 13 sts of ribbing panel, knit to end. Place first 84 (96, 110, 122, 134, 146) front sts onto holder. Make a note of the chart rnd just completed so you can resume working the front sts later with the correct row.

back

Work 86 (98, 110, 122, 134, 146) back sts back and forth in rows as foll:

NEXT ROW: (WS) Sl 1, k3, purl to last 4 sts, k4.

DEC ROW 1: (RS) Work according to your size as foll:

SIZES 29¾ (33¼)" ONLY

Sl 1, k3, ssk, knit to last 6 sts, k2tog, k4—2 sts dec'd.

SIZE 37¼" ONLY

Sl 1, k3, sssk (see Glossary), knit to last 7 sts, k3tog, k4—4 sts dec'd.

SIZES (40¾, 44½, 48)" ONLY

Sl 1, k3, sssk (see Glossary), ssk, knit to last 9 sts, k2tog, k3tog, k4—6 sts dec'd.

Rep the last 2 rows once, then work 1 more WS row as established—82 (94, 102, 110, 122, 134) sts.

ALL SIZES

DEC ROW 2: Cont according to your size as foll:

SIZE 29¾" ONLY

Do not work these dec instructions; skip to All sizes below.

SIZES (33¼, 37¼)" ONLY

Sl 1, k3, ssk, knit to last 6 sts, k2tog, k4—2 sts dec'd. Work 1 WS row as established, then rep the last 2 rows (2, 5) more times—(88, 90) sts.

SIZES (40¾, 44½, 48)" ONLY

Sl 1, k3, sssk, knit to last 7 sts, k3tog, k4—4 sts dec'd. Work 1 WS row as established, the rep the last 2 rows (3, 6, 8) more times—(94, 94, 98) sts.

Terre Hill

7-st repeat
work 9 (9, 9, 10, 10, 10) times

☐ knit on RS rows and all rnds; purl on WS rows

◉ yo

╱ k2tog on RS rows and all rnds; p2tog on WS rows

╲ ssk on RS rows and all rnds; p2tog tbl on WS rows

☐ pattern repeat

ALL SIZES

Work even on 82 (88, 90, 94, 94, 98) sts until armholes measure 6½ (7¼, 8¼, 8¾, 9, 9½)" (16.5 [18.5, 21, 22, 23, 24] cm), ending with a WS row.

Knit 6 rows, ending with a WS row—armholes measure 7 (7¾, 8¾, 9¼, 9½, 10)" (18 [19.5, 22, 23.5, 24, 25.5] cm).

NEXT ROW: (RS) K13 (13, 14, 14, 14, 15), BO center 56 (62, 62, 66, 66, 68) sts, knit to end—13 (13, 14, 14, 14, 15) sts rem each side. Place shoulder sts onto separate holders.

front

note: *When working the chart back and forth in rows, even-numbered chart rows are WS rows; odd-numbered chart rows are RS rows.*

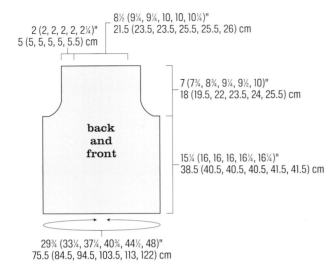

2 (2, 2, 2, 2, 2¼)"
5 (5, 5, 5, 5, 5.5) cm

8½ (9¼, 9¼, 10, 10, 10¼)"
21.5 (23.5, 23.5, 25.5, 25.5, 26) cm

7 (7¾, 8¾, 9¼, 9½, 10)"
18 (19.5, 22, 23.5, 24, 25.5) cm

back
and
front

15¼ (16, 16, 16, 16¼, 16¼)"
38.5 (40.5, 40.5, 40.5, 41.5, 41.5) cm

29¾ (33¼, 37¼, 40¾, 44½, 48)"
75.5 (84.5, 94.5, 103.5, 113, 122) cm

Return 84 (96, 110, 122, 134, 146)
held front sts to needle and rejoin
yarn with WS facing.

NEXT ROW: (WS) Sl 1, k3, work in patt
to last 4 sts, k4.

DEC ROW 1: (RS) Work according to
your size as foll:

SIZES 29¾ (33¼)" ONLY

Sl 1, k3, ssk, work in patt to last
6 sts, k2tog, k4—2 sts dec'd.

SIZE 37¼" ONLY

Sl 1, k3, sssk, work in patt to last
7 sts, k3tog, k4—4 sts dec'd.

SIZES (40¾, 44½, 48)" ONLY

Sl 1, k3, sssk, ssk, work in patt to
last 9 sts, k2tog, k3tog, k4—6 sts
dec'd.

ALL SIZES

Rep the last 0 (2, 2, 2, 2, 2) rows 0
(1, 1, 1, 1, 1) time(s), then work 1 WS
row as established—82 (92, 102, 110,
122, 134) sts.

DEC ROW 2: Cont according to your size
as foll:

SIZE 29¾" ONLY

Do not work these dec instructions;
skip to All sizes below.

SIZES (33¼, 37¼)" ONLY

Sl 1, k3, ssk, knit to last 6 sts, k2tog,
k4—2 sts dec'd. Work 1 WS row as
established, then rep the last 2 rows
(1, 5) more time(s)—(88, 90) sts.

SIZES (40¾, 44½, 48)" ONLY

Sl 1, k3, sssk, knit to last 7 sts,
k3tog, k4—4 sts dec'd. Work 1 WS
row as established, the rep the last
2 rows (3, 6, 8) more times—(94, 94,
98) sts.

ALL SIZES

Work even on 82 (88, 90, 94, 94,
98) sts until armholes measure 6½
(7¼, 8¼, 8¾, 9, 9½)" (16.5 [18.5, 21,
22, 23, 24] cm), ending with a WS
row.

Knit 6 rows, ending with a WS
row—armholes measure 7 (7¾, 8¾,
9¼, 9½, 10)" (18 [19.5, 22, 23.5, 24,
25.5] cm).

NEXT ROW: (RS) K13 (13, 14, 14, 14, 15),
BO center 56 (62, 62, 66, 66, 68) sts,
knit to end—13 (13, 14, 14, 14, 15) sts
rem each side. Place shoulder sts
onto separate holders.

finishing

With yarn threaded on a tapestry
needle, use the Kitchener st (see
Glossary) to join the front and back
at the shoulders.

Block to measurements. Weave in
loose ends.

Swatara
socks

Worked from the top down, these lacy socks feature leaf and arrow patterns. The arrow lace panels run along the sides of the leg, then they split gracefully at the round heel gusset so that half of each panel continues along the sides of the heel flap (which is worked in the eye-of-the-partridge pattern). The other half of each panel travels along the side of the instep. The directional leaf motif is centered on both the back and front of the leg in mirror images on the two socks. The socks finish with a classic wedge toe and Kitchener stitch.

finished size

About 7 (7¾)" (18 [19.5] cm) sock foot circumference, unstretched, to fit up to 8½ (9½)" (21.5 [24] cm) foot circumference; 8½ (9)" (21.5 [23] cm) foot length from back of heel to tip of toe, unstretched; and 5¾" (14.5 cm) leg length from CO to start of heel flap for both sizes.

Socks shown to fit 8½" (21.5 cm) foot circumference.

yarn

Fingering weight (#1 Super Fine).

Shown here: The Alpaca Yarn Company Paca Peds (65% superwash wool, 20% alpaca, 15% nylon; 360 yd [329 m]/100 g): #630 Tree Frog, 1 skein for both sizes.

needles

Size U.S. 1 (2.25 mm): set of 4 double-pointed (dpn), or two 24" (60 cm) circular (cir), or one 40" (100 cm) cir (to work the magic-loop method).

Adjust needle size if necessary to obtain the correct gauge.

notions

Markers (m); tapestry needle.

gauge

39 sts and 57 rnds = 4" (10 cm) in lace patts from charts and St st, unstretched, worked in rnds.

NOTES

- The center back and front lace panels are mirror images of each other; therefore separate charts are used for the right and left socks. In the phototgraphs, the model is wearing the socks on the opposite feet.

- Rounds 1–6 of each chart are set-up rounds. Work these set-up rounds once, then repeat the indicated rounds for the pattern; do not repeat the set-up rounds.

- Leg and foot length are adjustable, but longer socks in the larger size may require an extra skein of yarn.

STITCH GUIDE

1×1 TWISTED RIB (multiple of 2 sts)

All rnds: *K1 through back loop (tbl), p1tbl; rep from *.

right sock

CO 68 (76) sts. Divide the sts on your choice of needles so there are 34 (38) sts designated for the front of the leg and 34 (38) sts designated for the back of the leg. Place marker (pm) and join for working in rnds, being careful not to twist sts; rnd begins at outside of leg, at start of front-of-leg sts.

Work in 1×1 twisted rib (see Stitch Guide) until piece measures 1" (2.5 cm) from CO.

leg

Work according to your size as foll:

SIZE 7" ONLY

NEXT RND: *P1, work Rnd 1 of **SWATARA RIGHT ARROW CHART** over 4 sts, p1, work Rnd 1 of **SWATARA RIGHT FOOT CHART** over 23 sts, p1, work Rnd 1 of **SWATARA LEFT ARROW CHART** over 4 sts; rep from * once more.

SIZE 7¾" ONLY

NEXT RND: *P1, work Rnd 1 of **SWATARA RIGHT ARROW CHART** over 4 sts, p1, k1tbl, p1, work Rnd 1 of **SWATARA RIGHT FOOT CHART** over 23 sts, p1, k1tbl, p1, work Rnd 1 of **SWATARA LEFT ARROW CHART** over 4 sts; rep from * once more.

BOTH SIZES

Working sts between chart patts as they appear (purl the purls and knit any k1tbl's through the back loops), cont in established patts for 67 more rnds for both sizes, ending with Rnd 12 of foot chart and Rnd 8 of arrow charts—68 chart rnds completed; leg measures about 5¾" (14.5 cm) from CO.

Swatara Right Foot

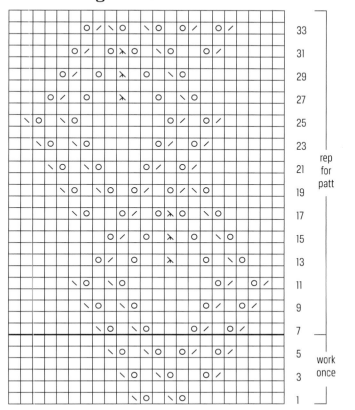

33
31
29
27
25
23
21
19
17
15
13
11
9
7
5
3
1

rep for patt

work once

23-st panel

Swatara Right Arrow

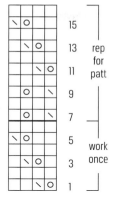

15
13 rep for patt
11
9
7
5 work once
3
1

4-st panel

Swatara Left Arrow

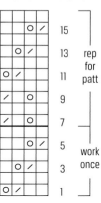

15
13 rep for patt
11
9
7
5 work once
3
1

4-st panel

	knit on RS rows and all rnds; purl on WS rows
$\boxed{\circ}$	yo
$\boxed{/}$	k2tog
$\boxed{\backslash}$	ssk
$\boxed{\lambda}$	sl 1, k2tog, psso

note: *For a longer leg, work more rnds here, ending with an even-numbered rnd; every 4 rnds added will lengthen the leg by about ¼" (6 mm).*

heel

SET-UP RND: (Rnd 13 of foot chart; Rnd 9 of arrow charts) Remove m, p1, replace m, work 33 (37) front-of-leg sts in established patts—35 (39) back-of-leg sts rem unworked; front-of-leg sts are now arranged with a 4-st arrow patt at each side.

note: *If you adjusted the leg length, make a note of the chart rounds just completed so you can resume the patterns with the correct round later.*

HEEL FLAP

The heel is worked back and forth on 35 (39) back-of-leg sts; the 33 (37) front-of-leg sts will be joined later for instep. Work the odd-numbered rows of the arrow charts as RS rows; work the even-numbered rows as WS rows.

Swatara Left Foot

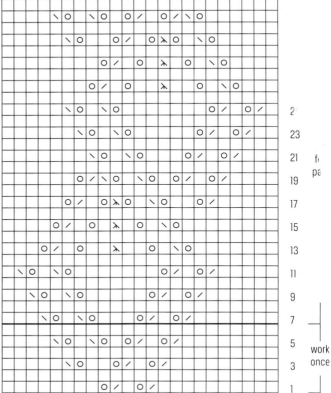

23-st panel

	knit on RS rows and all rnds; purl on WS rows
☐	knit on RS rows and all rnds; purl on WS rows
○	yo
╱	k2tog
╲	ssk
丬	sl 1, k2tog, psso

With RS still facing, cont on heel sts for your size as foll:

SIZE 7" ONLY

ROW 1: (RS) Sl 1 purlwise with yarn in back (wyb), work 4 sts of **SWATARA RIGHT ARROW CHART** as established, p1, [sl 1 purlwise wyb, k1] 11 times, sl 1 purlwise wyb, p1, work 4 sts of **SWATARA LEFT ARROW CHART** as established, p1.

ROW 2: (WS) Sl 1 knitwise with yarn in front (wyf), p4, k1, p23, k1, p4, k1.

ROW 3: Sl 1 purlwise wyb, work 4 sts of **SWATARA RIGHT ARROW CHART** as established, p1, [k1, sl 1 purlwise wyb] 11 times, k1, p1, work 4 sts of **SWATARA LEFT ARROW CHART** as established, p1.

ROW 4: Rep Row 2.

Rep these 4 rows 8 more times— 36 heel flap rows completed.

SIZE 7¾" ONLY

ROW 1: (RS) Sl 1 purlwise with yarn in back (wyb), work 4 sts of **SWATARA RIGHT ARROW CHART** as established, p1, k1tbl, p1, [sl 1 purlwise wyb, k1] 11 times, sl 1 purlwise wyb, p1, k1tbl, p1, work 4 sts of **SWATARA LEFT ARROW CHART** as established, p1.

ROW 2: (WS) Sl 1 knitwise with yarn in front (wyf), p4, k1, p1tbl, k1, p23, k1, p1tbl, k1, p4, k1.

ROW 3: Sl 1 purlwise wyb, work 4 sts of **SWATARA RIGHT ARROW CHART** as established, p1, k1tbl, p1, [k1, sl 1 purlwise wyb] 11 times, k1, p1, k1tbl, p1, work 4 sts of **SWATARA LEFT ARROW CHART** as established, p1.

ROW 4: Rep Row 2.

Rep these 4 rows 10 more times—44 heel flap rows completed.

HEEL TURN

Work short-rows as foll:

ROW 1: (RS) Sl 1, k19 (21), ssk, k1, turn work.

ROW 2: (WS) Sl 1, p6, p2tog, p1, turn work.

ROW 3: Sl 1, knit to 1 st before gap formed on previous RS row, ssk (1 st each side of gap), k1, turn work.

ROW 4: Sl 1, purl to 1 st before gap formed on previous WS row, p2tog (1 st each side of gap), p1, turn work.

Rep Rows 3 and 4 until 21 (23) sts rem, ending with WS Row 4.

NEXT ROW: (RS) Sl 1, knit to end of heel sts.

SHAPE GUSSETS

JOINING RND: With RS facing, pick up and knit 19 (21) sts along the left side of the heel flap, pm for new beg of rnd at start of instep sts, pick up and purl 1 st in corner, work 33 (37) instep sts in established patts, pick up and purl 1 st in corner, pick up and knit 19 (21) sts along the right side of the heel flap, then knit across 21 (23) heel flap sts to end at m—94 (104) sts total; 35 (39) instep sts with new picked-up purl st at each side; 59 (65) gusset and sole sts.

RND 1: Work 35 (39) instep sts in established patts, k1, ssk, knit to last 3 sts, k2tog, k1—2 sts dec'd.

RND 2: Work 35 (39) sts in established patts, knit to end of rnd.

Rep Rnds 1 and 2 until 68 (76) sts rem—35 (39) instep sts; 33 (37) sole sts.

foot

Working sole sts in St st, cont working instep sts in established patts until foot measures 7 (7¼)" (18 [18.5] cm) from center back heel or 1½ (1¾)" (3.8 [4.5] cm) less than desired total length, ending with an even-numbered chart rnd.

toe

Remove m, p1, replace m—34 (38) sts each for top and bottom of foot.

RND 1: *K1, ssk, k28 (32), k2tog, k1, pm; rep from *—4 sts dec'd.

RND 2: Knit.

RND 3: *K1, ssk, knit to 3 sts before m, k2tog, k1; rep from *—4 sts dec'd.

Rep Rnds 2 and 3 until 24 (28) sts rem—12 (14) sts each for top and bottom foot; toe measures about 1½ (1¾)" (3.8 [4.5] cm) from last chart rnd.

Arrange sts with 12 (14) sts each on 2 needles if they are not already on 2 needles. Cut yarn, leaving a 12" (30.5 cm) tail. Thread tail on a tapestry needle and use the Kitchener st (see Glossary) to graft the sts tog.

finishing

Weave in loose ends. Block according to directions in sidebar at right, if desired.

left sock

CO 68 (76) sts and work in 1×1 twisted rib as for right sock until piece measures 1" (2.5 cm) from CO; rnd begins at inside of leg, at start of front-of-leg sts.

leg

Work according to your size as foll:

SIZE 7" ONLY

NEXT RND: *P1, work Rnd 1 of **SWATARA RIGHT ARROW CHART** over 4 sts, p1, work Rnd 1 of **SWATARA LEFT FOOT CHART** over 23 sts, p1, work Rnd 1 of **SWATARA LEFT ARROW CHART** over 4 sts; rep from * once more.

SIZE 7¾" ONLY

NEXT RND: *P1, work Rnd 1 of **SWATARA RIGHT ARROW CHART** over 4 sts, p1, k1tbl, p1, work Rnd 1 of **SWATARA LEFT FOOT CHART** over 23 sts, p1, k1tbl, p1, work Rnd 1 of **SWATARA LEFT ARROW CHART** over 4 sts; rep from * once more.

BOTH SIZES

Compete as for right sock.

MAKING A SOCK BLOCKER

I rarely block socks that I knit for myself, even ones with lace patterns. I find that they block themselves as I wear them. But if you want to give lace socks as a gift, you'll want to block them so they look their best. Although you can purchase sock blockers, you can easily make your own out of stiff cardboard.

To begin, flatten the finished sock on a piece of cardboard, then use a pen or pencil to trace around the sock, making an outline that is slightly bigger than the sock itself. Carefully cut out the traced sock shape, then insert the form into your sock. Because the form is slightly larger than the sock, it will cause the stitches to stretch slightly to reveal the beautiful lace pattern.

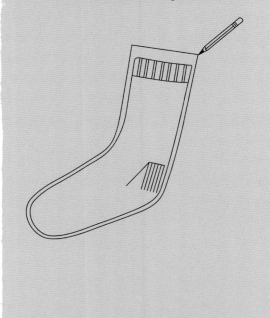

Millway
socks

These beautiful lace socks look much more complicated to knit than they are. Worked from the toe up, they feature a reverse gusset and slipped-stitch heel flap. The toe-up construction allows you to knit the feet without worrying about running out of yarn and then work the legs until the yarn runs out. The cuff at the top is finished with a pretty picot hem.

finished size

About 7 (8)" (18 [20.5]cm) sock foot circumference, unstretched, to fit up to 8¾ (9½)" (22 [24]cm) foot circumference; 9 (9½)" (23 [24]cm) foot length from back of heel to tip of toe, unstretched; 5¼" (13.5cm) leg length for both sizes from top of heel flap to edge of finished hem at top of leg.

Socks shown to fit 8¾" (22cm) foot circumference.

yarn

Fingering weight (#1 Super Fine).

Shown here: Baah! LaJolla (100% merino; 400 yd [366 m]/100 g): Orange Amber, 1 skein for both sizes.

needles

Size U.S. 1 (2.25 mm): set of 5 double-pointed (dpn), or two 24" (60cm) circular (cir), or one 40" (100cm) cir (to work in the magic-loop method).

Adjust needle size if necessary to obtain the correct gauge.

notions

Markers (m); tapestry needle.

gauge

39 sts and 48 rnds = 4" (10cm) in St st, unstretched and worked in rnds; 36.5 sts and 48 rnds = 4" (10cm) in lace patt from Millway chart, unstretched and worked in rnds.

NOTES

- The leg and foot lengths are adjustable, but longer socks in the larger size may require an extra skein of yarn.
- Work each blue-shaded symbol of the **MILLWAY CHART** as p1 for the smaller size and as p2 for the larger size. On the instep, the chart is worked a multiple of 16 stitches plus 1 for the smaller size, and a multiple of 18 stitches plus 2 for the larger size. For the leg, the chart is worked as a multiple of 16 (18) stitches, without the balancing stitch(es) at the end of the chart.

toe

Using Judy's Magic Cast-On method (see Glossary), CO 22 (24) sts.

Divide the sts between needles so that 11 (12) sts are designated for the top of the foot and 11 (12) sts are designated for the sole.

RND 1: Knit.

RND 2: *K1, M1 (see Glossary), k9 (10), M1, k1, place marker (pm); rep from * once more—4 sts inc'd total; 2 sts inc'd each for top of foot and sole.

RND 3: Knit.

RND 4: *K1, M1, knit to 1 st before m, M1, k1, slip marker (sl m); rep from * once more—4 sts inc'd.

Rep Rnds 3 and 4 nine (eleven) more times—66 (76) sts; 33 (38) sts each for top of foot and sole.

Knit 1 rnd even—toe measures about 2 (2¼)" (5 [5.5] cm) from CO.

foot

NEXT RND: For the 33 (38) instep sts on top of foot, work the 16 (18)-st patt rep from Rnd 1 of **MILLWAY CHART** 2 times, then work the 1 (2) st(s) at the end of the chart once; sl m, then knit 33 (38) sole sts to end of rnd.

Cont in established patts until foot measures 6 (6½)" (15 [16.5] cm) from CO, or 3" (7.5 cm) less than desired total foot length (see Notes).

gusset

RND 1: Work 33 (38) insteps sts in patt, sl m, k1, M1, knit to 1 st before m, M1, k1—2 gusset sts inc'd on sole of foot.

Millway

(chart with 24 rows, numbered 1–23 on odd rows)

16 (18)-st repeat
See Notes for blue-shaded sts.

☐ knit	╱ k2tog
• purl 1 (2); see Notes	╲ ssk
○ yo	☐ pattern repeat

RND 2: Work 33 (38) instep sts in patt, sl m, knit to end of rnd.

Cont for your size as foll.

SIZE 7" ONLY

Rep the last 2 rnds 10 more times—55 sole sts; foot measures about 7¾" (19.5 cm) from CO.

SIZE 8" ONLY

Rep Rnds 1 and 2 nine more times, work Rnd 1 once more, then work 1 more rnd in patt inc only 1 st at the beg of the sole sts—61 sole sts; foot measures about 8¼" (21 cm) from CO.

BOTH SIZES

Work 33 (38) instep sts in patt and stop. Make a note of the chart row just completed so you can resume the patt later with the correct row.

heel

The heel is worked back and forth on 55 (61) sole sts; the 33 (38) instep sts will be joined later for the front of the leg.

TURN HEEL

Work short-rows (see Glossary) as foll:

ROW 1: (RS) K37 (41), k1f&b (see Glossary), k1, wrap next st, turn work—40 (44) worked sts, 16 (18) unworked sts; wrapped st is next to turning gap.

ROW 2: (WS) P22 (24), p1f&b (see Glossary), p1, wrap next st, turn work—25 (27) worked sts in center, 16 (18) unworked sts at each side; wrapped sts are next to turning gap at each side.

ROW 3: K20 (22), k1f&b, k1, wrap next st, turn work.

ROW 4: P18 (20), p1f&b, p1, wrap next st, turn work.

ROW 5: K16 (18), k1f&b, k1, wrap next st, turn work.

ROW 6: P14 (16), p1f&b, p1, wrap next st, turn work.

ROW 7: K12 (14), k1f&b, k1, wrap next st, turn work.

ROW 8: P10 (12), p1f&b, p1, wrap next st, turn work—63 (69) heel sts total; 4 wrapped sts at each side.

HEEL FLAP

NEXT ROW: (RS) With RS facing, knit to end of sole sts, working wraps tog with wrapped sts when you come to them, then work across 33 (38) instep sts in established patt.

Work heel flap back and forth in rows on sole sts while dec gusset sts as foll:

ROW 1: (RS) K47 (52), working rem wraps tog with wrapped sts when you come to them, ssk, turn work.

ROW 2: (WS) *Sl 1, p31 (35), p2tog, turn work.

ROW 3: [Sl 1, k1] 16 (18) times, ssk, turn work.

Rep Rows 2 and 3 until 33 (37) heel sts rem, ending with WS Row 2.

NEXT ROW: (RS) Ssk, knit to last 2 (3) heel sts, k2tog (k3tog)—31 (34) heel sts rem; 33 (38) instep sts; 64 (72) sts total.

leg

The heel sts now become the back-of-leg sts; the instep sts now become the front-of-leg sts; rnd begins at side of leg at start of front-of-leg sts.

NEXT RND: Cont in established lace patt, work 16 (18)-st patt rep of chart 4 times around; do not work the 1 (2) balancing st(s) at end of chart.

Cont in established patt until leg measures 4¾" (12 cm) from top of heel flap or ½" (1.3 cm) less than desired total length.

cuff

Knit 6 rnds even.

PICOT FOLD LINE: *Yo, k2tog; rep from *—leg measures about 5¼" (13.5 cm) from top of heel flap.

Knit 5 rnds even for cuff facing.

BO all sts. Cut yarn, leaving an 18" (45.5 cm) tail.

finishing

Fold cuff facing to WS along picot fold line. Thread tail on a tapestry needle and use a whipstitch (see Glossary) to tack the BO edge in place.

Weave in loose ends. Block if desired.

Strasburg
arm warmers

Long and exquisitely soft, these arm warmers are designed to keep you toasty in knitterly style. Bold lace panels jazz up the simple design that includes ribbing for a snug and comfortable fit. Wear them with short sleeves when the temperatures begin to fall or under your winter coat for extra warmth on especially blustery days.

finished size

About 10 (11, 12)" (25.5 [28, 30.5] cm) upper arm and hand circumference and 18" (45.5 cm) long.

Arm warmers shown measure 10" (25.5 cm).

yarn

Worsted weight (#4 Medium).

Shown here: Dream in Color Classy with Cashmere (70% superwash merino, 20% cashmere, 10% nylon; 210 yd [192 m]/4 oz [113 g]): Malibu Sail, 2 (3, 3) skeins.

needles

Size U.S. 6 (4 mm): set of 4 or 5 double-pointed (dpn).

Adjust needle size if necessary to obtain the correct gauge.

notions

Markers (m); stitch holder; tapestry needle.

gauge

20 sts and 32 rnds = 4" (10 cm) in k3, p1 rib worked in rnds, slightly stretched so p1 columns appear 1 st wide; 19 sts of lace panel from strasburg chart measure 3½" (9 cm) wide.

NOTES

— To adjust arm length, work more or fewer repeats of the 16-round lace pattern before starting the thumb gusset; every repeat added or removed will lengthen or shorten the piece by about 2" (5 cm).

— To make leg warmers, omit the thumb gusset and add more 4-stitch repeats of the k3, p1 rib pattern to increase the circumference as necessary. Every 4 rib stitches added or removed will increase or decrease the circumference by about ¾" (2 cm).

STITCH GUIDE

MOCK CABLE (worked over 3 sts)

Use the right needle tip to lift the third st on the left needle over the first and second sts and off the needle, then work the first and second sts on left needle as k1, yo, k1—3 sts made from 3 sts.

left arm warmer

CO 52 (56, 60) sts. Arrange sts as evenly as possible on 3 or 4 dpn. Place marker (pm) and join for working in rnds, being careful not to twist sts.

NEXT RND: *K3, p1; rep from *.

Rep the last rnd until piece measures 1" (2.5 cm) from CO.

SET-UP RND: Work Rnd 1 of STRASBURG CHART over 19 sts, p1, [k3, p1] 8 (9, 10) times.

Working sts outside lace panel in established rib, cont in patt until Rnds 1–16 of chart have been worked a total of 6 times, or for desired length (see Notes)—96 chart rnds completed; piece measures about 13" (33 cm) from CO.

SHAPE THUMB GUSSET

RND 1: Work Rnd 1 of chart over 19 sts, p1, [k3, p1] 6 (7, 8) times, k3, pm, p1, pm, k3, p1—1 st between new gusset markers.

RND 2: Work in established patts to first gusset m, slip marker (sl m), M1R purlwise (see Glossary), k1, M1L purlwise (see Glossary), sl second gusset m, work in patt to end— 2 gusset sts inc'd.

RNDS 3, 4, AND 5: Work in established patts to gusset m, sl m, p1, knit to 1 st before next gusset m, p1, sl m, work in patt to end.

RND 6: Work in established patts to gusset m, M1R purlwise, knit to next gusset m, M1L purlwise, sl second gusset m, work in patt to end—2 gusset sts inc'd.

Rep Rnds 3–6 only 3 (4, 5) more times, ending with Rnd 2 (6, 10) of chart —11 (13 15) gusset sts; 62 (68, 74) sts total.

DIVIDE FOR THUMB

NEXT RND: (Rnd 3 [7, 11] of chart) Work in patt to first gusset m, remove m, place 11 (13, 15) gusset sts onto holder, remove m, use the backward-loop method (see Glossary) to CO 1 st over gap, work in patt to end—52 (56, 60) sts rem.

HAND

Cont in established patts, work 13 (9, 5) more rnds to end with Rnd 16 of chart—128 total chart rnds and 8 complete 16-rnd chart reps; piece measures 17" (43 cm) from CO.

NEXT RND: *K3, p1; rep from *.

Rep the last rnd for 1" (2.5 cm)— piece measures 18" (45.5 cm) from CO.

BO all sts in patt.

THUMB

Place 11 (13, 15) held thumb gusset sts as evenly spaced as possible on 3 dpn.

Join yarn to beg of sts with RS facing, [k3, p1] 2 (3, 3) times, k3 (1, 3), then pick up and knit 1 st from st CO across thumb gap—12 (14, 16) sts total.

Pm and join for working in rnds.

NEXT RND: [K3, p1] 3 (3, 4) times, then work [k1, p1] 0 (1, 0) time(s).

Rep the last rnd until piece measures 1" (2.5 cm) from pick-up rnd.

BO all sts in patt.

Strasburg

19-st panel

□ knit	＼ ssk
⍉ k1tbl	⪢ k3tog
○ yo	⪡ sssk
／ k2tog	—○— mock cable (see Stitch Guide)

right arm warmer

CO 52 (56, 60) sts as work as for left armwarmer until 96 chart rnds have been completed, ending with Rnd 16 of chart—piece measures about 13" (33 cm) from CO.

SHAPE THUMB GUSSET

RND 1: Work Rnd 1 of chart over 19 sts, p1, k3, pm, p1, pm [k3, p1] 7 (8, 9) times—1 st between new gusset markers.

RND 2: Work in established patts to first gusset m, slip marker (sl m), M1R purlwise, k1, M1L purlwise, sl second gusset m, work in patt to end—2 gusset sts inc'd.

RNDS 3, 4, AND 5: Work in established patts to gusset m, sl m, p1, knit to 1 st before next gusset m, p1, sl m, work in patt to end.

RND 6: Work in established patts to gusset m, M1R purlwise, knit to next gusset m, M1L purlwise, sl second gusset m, work in patt to end—2 gusset sts inc'd.

Rep Rnds 3–6 only 3 (4, 5) more times, ending with Rnd 2 (6, 10) of chart —11 (13 15) gusset sts; 62 (68, 74) sts total.

DIVIDE FOR THUMB, HAND, AND THUMB

Work as for left arm warmer.

finishing

Weave in loose ends. Block if desired.

CHAPTER 4

Cold

Lace in the winter? Absolutely! Lace is perfect for dressing up accessories and sweaters. Used on just the hems or all over, lace adds texture, femininity, and class to any winter woolen. The projects in this chapter use heavier yarns and bold motifs that are sure to warm you up in the coldest months.

Cowls and hats are a must in the winter months. The lacy warmth of the AKRON COWL (page 86) will protect your neck from the coldest gusts winter can offer. The fashion-forward shapes and sophisticated lace patterning in the SALUNGA BERET (page 90) and MURRELL HAT (page 94) will top off your outerwear with style.

The BELLEMONT CARDIGAN (page 98), ENGLESIDE COWL-NECK PULLOVER (page 114), and MANHEIM FITTED PULLOVER (page 122) are designed for layering during the snowy season. Warm and woolly, these sweaters feature graceful eyelet panels, lace trimmed hems, and bold allover patterns.

Akron
cowl

Texture and eyelets create a fun pattern in this neck warmer. Simple lace and clever decreases make the garter-stitch block appear to tilt. This is a perfect pattern for the novice lace knitter. Knit it with a special skein of super-soft yarn and you won't want to take it off.

finished size
About 24" (61 cm) in circumference and 8" (20.5 cm) tall.

yarn
DK weight (#3 Light).

Shown here: Madelinetosh Tosh DK (100% superwash merino; 225 yd [206 m]/100 g): Antique Lace, 1 skein.

needles
Size U.S. 7 (4.5 mm): 24" (60 cm) circular (cir).

Adjust needle size if necessary to obtain the correct gauge.

notions
Markers (m); tapestry needle.

gauge
20 sts and 32 rnds = 4" (10 cm) in patt from Akron chart, worked in rnds.

STITCH GUIDE

4×1 RIB (multiple of 5 sts)

All rnds: *K4, p1; rep from *.

cowl

CO 120 sts. Place marker (pm) and join for working rnds, being careful not to twist sts.

Work in 4×1 rib (see Stitch Guide) until piece measures 1" (2.5 cm) from CO.

Work Rnds 1–16 of **AKRON CHART** 3 times—48 chart rnds total; piece measures about 7" (18 cm) from CO.

Work in 4×1 rib for 1" (2.5 cm)— piece measures 8" (20.5 cm) from CO.

Loosely BO all sts in patt.

finishing

Block to measurements. Weave in loose ends.

Akron

			knit
•		purl	
○		yo	
╱		k2tog	
╲		ssk	
		pattern repeat	

10-st repeat

Salunga
beret

A lightweight lace beret will keep you warm and stylish all winter. This hat starts with a circular cast-on at the top (this is a great technique for hats, shawls, or anything else that begins in the center of a circle); it ends with a tubular bind-off. The tubular bind-off is one of my favorite techniques—few techniques give me more satisfaction than one that's been perfectly executed. It's a bit time-consuming, but the clean look makes it worth the effort.

finished size

About 21" (53.5 cm) head circumference, stretched.

yarn

Fingering weight (#1 Super Fine).

Shown here: Spud & Chloe Fine (80% superwash wool, 20% silk; 248 yd [227 m]/65 g): #7818 Green Bean, 1 skein.

needles

Size U.S. 3 (3.25 mm): 16" (40 cm) circular (cir) and set of 4 double-pointed (dpn).

Adjust needle size if necessary to obtain the correct gauge.

notions

Markers (m); tapestry needle; smooth, contrasting waste yarn and 10" to 11" (25.5 to 28 cm) diameter dinner plate for blocking.

gauge

28 sts and 40 rnds = 4" (10 cm) average gauge in lace patts from charts, worked in rnds.

STITCH GUIDE
SALUNGA BODY CHART, BLUE-SHADED STITCHES

In order to keep the pattern properly aligned, it will be necessary to "borrow" 1 stitch from the end of the previous round to work the double decrease at the start of Rnds 46, 48, 50, 58, and 66 (shaded in blue on the chart). Prepare for each "loan" by knitting the previous round to the last stitch, temporarily slip the last stitch (shaded in blue) to the right needle, remove the marker, return the slipped stitch to the left needle, and replace the marker. Work the blue-shaded double decrease at the start of the following round over the "borrowed" stitch and the next 2 stitches after it.

Salunga Crown

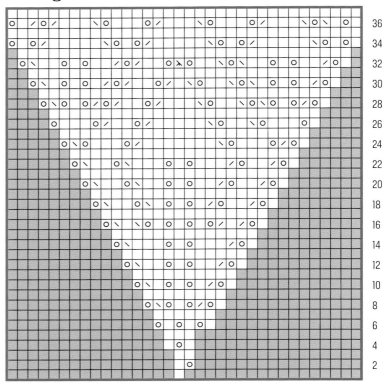

1-st repeat inc'd to 34-st repeat

crown

With dpn and using Emily Ocker's method (see Glossary), CO 5 sts.

Arrange sts on 3 dpn, place marker (pm), and join for working in rnds, being careful not to twist sts.

Work Rnds 1–37 of **SALUNGA CROWN CHART**, working each chart row 5 times in each rnd, increasing as shown, and changing to cir needle when there are too many sts to fit comfortably on dpn—170 sts; 34 sts each patt rep.

☐	knit
⊙	yo
╱	k2tog
╲	ssk
⅄	sl 1, k2tog, psso
▨	no stitch
☐	see Stitch Guide
☐	pattern repeat

Salunga Body

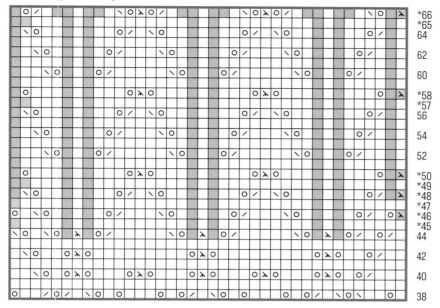

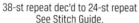

38-st repeat dec'd to 24-st repeat
See Stitch Guide.

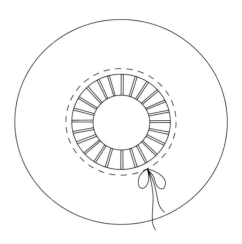

Thread contrasting yarn through the top of the ribbing
to prevent it from stretching while the lace is blocked.

body

NEXT RND: Work Row 38 of **SALUNGA BODY CHART** 5 times around, inc each 34-st patt rep to a 38-st patt rep as shown—190 sts.

Work Rnds 39–66 of chart (see Stitch Guide), decreasing as shown—120 sts rem; 24 sts each patt rep.

Knit 1 rnd even.

NEXT RND: *K1, p1; rep from * to end.

Rep the last rnd until rib measures 1" (2.5 cm).

Use the tubular k1, p1 method (see Glossary) to BO all sts.

finishing

Run a strand of smooth waste yarn threaded on a tapestry needle through the boundary between the body and ribbing. Wash the beret according to the instructions on the ball band, then insert the blocking plate into the damp beret. Pull on the waste yarn to prevent the ribbed brim from stretching while the lace pattern is stretched around the plate. Set the plate on top of a mug or canister so that air can flow freely on all sides. Allow to air-dry thoroughly before removing the plate.

Weave in loose ends.

Murrell
hat

Although this slouchy hat is lacy, the inherent warmth in the alpaca yarn will keep you toasty throughout the chilly months. If you'd like a slightly different shape, you can cast on an extra repeat for more dramatic slouch or cast on one less repeat for a close-fitting beanie. Because the alpaca yarn is available in sixty beautiful colors, you can knit a hat to match every piece in your winter wardrobe!

finished size

About 19¼ (21½, 24)" (49 [54.5, 61] cm) head circumference.

Hat shown measures 21½" (54.5 cm) in circumference.

yarn

DK weight (#3 Light).

Shown here: The Alpaca Yarn Company Classic Alpaca (100% baby alpaca; 110 yd [101 m]/50 g): #1800 Ozark Purple, 2 skeins (all sizes).

needles

Ribbing: size U.S. 4 (3.5 mm): 16" (40 cm) circular (cir).

Body: size U.S. 5 (3.75 mm): 16" (40 cm) cir and set of 4 or 5 double-pointed (dpn).

Adjust needle size if necessary to obtain the correct gauge.

notions

Markers (m); tapestry needle.

gauge

20 sts and 32 rnds = 4" (10 cm) in lace patt from Murrell Body chart, worked in rnds on larger needles.

brim

With smaller cir needle, CO 96 (108, 120) sts. Place marker (pm) and join for working in rnds, being careful not to twist sts.

NEXT RND: *K2, p2; rep from *.

Rep the last rnd until piece measures 2" (5 cm) from CO.

body

Change to larger cir needle. Work Rnds 1–16 of **MURRELL BODY CHART** 3 times, working the 6-st patt rep 16 (18, 20) times in each rnd—48 chart rnds completed; piece measures about 8" (20.5 cm) from CO.

crown

Work Rnds 1–18 of **MURRELL CROWN CHART**, working the 12-st patt rep 8 (9, 10) times in each rnd and changing to dpn when there are too few sts to fit comfortably on cir needle—8 (9, 10) sts rem.

Cut yarn, leaving an 8" (20.5 cm) tail. Thread tail on a tapestry needle, draw through rem sts, pull tight to close hole, and secure on WS.

finishing

Block to measurements. Weave in loose ends.

Murrell Crown

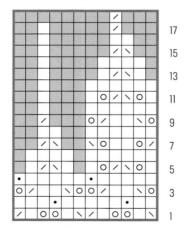

12-st repeat
dec'd to 1-st repeat

Murrell Body

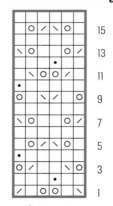

6-st repeat

☐	knit
•	purl
○	yo
╱	k2tog
╲	ssk
▨	no stitch
☐	pattern repeat

Bellemont
cardigan

This top-down raglan features a deep square neckline and graceful lace panels along each side of the front opening and along the center of each sleeve. Delicate picot hems add to the sweetly feminine look. Worked seamlessly in one piece, you'll enjoy knitting this cardigan as much as you'll enjoy wearing it!

finished size

About 36½ (40½, 44½, 48½, 52½, 56½)" (92.5 [103, 113, 123, 133.5, 143.5] cm) bust circumference, including 1" (2.5 cm) front band. Sweater shown measures 36½" (92.5 cm).

yarn

Worsted weight (#4 Medium).

Shown here: Swans Island Natural Colors Collection Merino Worsted (100% organic merino; 250 yd [229 m]/100 g): #YW207 Indigo, 5 (6, 6, 7, 8, 8) skeins.

needles

Size U.S. 8 (5 mm): 24" (60 cm) and 32" (80 cm) circular (cir) and set of 4 or 5 double-pointed (dpn).

Adjust needle size if necessary to obtain the correct gauge.

notions

Markers (m; 4 in raglan color and 8 in a different color for lace panels); tapestry needle; six ¾" (2 cm) buttons.

gauge

20 sts and 28 rows/rnds = 4" (10 cm) in St st and lace patts from charts.

yoke

With shorter cir needle, CO 1 st for left front, place marker in raglan color (pm), CO 17 (17, 17, 19, 23, 25) sts for left sleeve, pm, CO 33 (37, 43, 47, 55, 61) sts for back, pm, CO 17 (17, 17, 19, 23, 25) sts for right sleeve, pm, CO 1 st for right front—69 (73, 79, 87, 103, 113) sts total.

NEXT ROW: (WS) Purl, using markers in lace panel color to mark the center 15 sts of each sleeve for lace patt—1 (1, 1, 2, 4, 5) sleeve st(s) on each side of marked 15-st chart section.

Work according to your size as foll, changing to longer cir needle when necessary.

SIZE 36½" ONLY

ROW 1: (RS) Sl 1, M1R (see Glossary), slip raglan marker (sl m), k1, M1L (see Glossary), sl chart m, work Row 1 of **BELLEMONT CHART B** over center 15 left sleeve sts, sl chart m, M1R, k1, sl m, M1L, knit across back sts to next m, M1R, sl m, k1, M1L, sl chart m, work Row 1 of **BELLEMONT CHART A** over center 15 right sleeve sts, sl chart m, M1R, k1, sl m, M1L, k1—8 sts inc'd; 1 st each front, 2 sts each for back and sleeves.

ROW 2: (WS) Sl 1, work in established patts, purling the last st and working new sts in St st.

ROW 3: Sl 1, knit to raglan m, M1R, sl m, *k1, M1L, knit to chart m, sl chart m, work 15 chart sts, sl chart m, knit to 1 st before m, M1R, k1,* sl m, M1L, knit across back sts to next m, M1R, sl m; rep from * to * for right sleeve, sl m, M1L, knit to end—8 sts inc'd; 1 st each front, 2 sts each for back and sleeves.

ROW 4: Sl 1, work in established patts to end of row.

ROWS 5 AND 6: Rep Rows 3 and 4 once more—93 sts; 4 sts each front, 39 back sts, 23 sts each sleeve.

ROW 7: Sl 1, p1, k1 through the back loop (tbl), p1, M1R, sl m, *k1, M1L, knit to chart m, sl chart m, work 15 chart sts, sl chart m, knit to 1 st before m, M1R, k1,* sl m, M1L, knit across back sts to next m, M1R, sl m; rep from * to * for right sleeve, sl m, M1L, p1, k1tbl, p1, k1—8 sts inc'd; 1 st each front, 2 sts each for back and sleeves.

ROW 8: Sl 1, work in established patts to end of row, working k1tbl sts as p1tbl on WS.

ROW 9: (body and sleeve inc row) Sl 1, p1, k1tbl, p1, knit to m, M1R, sl m, *k1, M1L, knit to chart m, sl chart m, work 15 chart sts, sl chart m, knit to 1 st before m, M1R, k1,* sl m, M1L, knit across back sts to next m, M1R, sl m; rep from * to * for right sleeve, sl m, M1L, knit to last 4 sts, p1, k1tbl, p1, k1—8 sts inc'd; 1 st each front, 2 sts each for back and sleeves.

ROW 10: Sl 1, work in established patts to end of row.

ROWS 11–27: Rep Rows 9 and 10 eight more times and then work Row 9 once more—181 sts; 15 sts each front, 61 back sts, 45 sleeve sts.

ROW 28: Sl 1, work in established patts to end of row.

ROW 29: (body only inc row) Sl 1, p1, k1tbl, p1, knit to m, M1R, sl m, *knit to chart m, sl chart m, work 15 chart sts, sl chart m, knit to next m,*

Bellemont Chart A

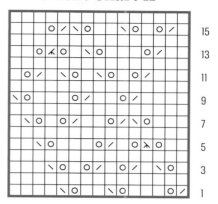

15-st repeat

Bellemont Chart B

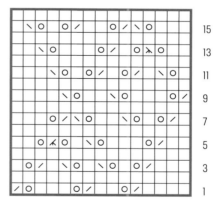

15-st repeat

☐ knit on RS rows and all rnds; purl on WS rows

⊡ yo

⟋ k2tog

⟍ ssk

⟑ k3tog

⅄ sssk

☐ pattern repeat

sl m, M1L, knit across back sts to next m, M1R, sl m, rep from * to * for right sleeve, sl m, M1L, knit to last 4 sts, p1, k1tbl, p1, k1—4 sts inc'd; 1 st each front, 2 back sts, no change to sleeve st count.

ROW 30: Sl 1, work in established patts to end of row.

ROW 31: (body and sleeve inc row) Rep Row 9—8 sts inc'd; 1 st each front, 2 sts each for back and sleeves.

ROW 32: Sl 1, work in established patts to end of row.

ROWS 33-36: Rep Rows 29–32 once more—205 sts; 19 sts each front, 69 back sts, 49 sleeve sts.

ROW 37: (body only inc row) Rep Row 29—209 sts; 20 sts each front, 71 back sts, 49 sleeve sts; yoke measures about 5½" (14 cm) from CO.

ROW 38: (WS) Use the backward-loop method (see Glossary) to CO 16 sts for right front neck. Beg by working across newly CO sts, p2, pm in chart color, p15, pm in chart color, k1, p1tbl, k1, work in established patts to last 4 sts, k1, p1tbl, k1, p1, then use the backward-loop method to CO 16 sts for left front neck—36 sts each front.

ROW 39: (body and sleeve inc row) Beg by working across newly CO sts, sl 1, k1, pm in chart color, work Row 1 of **BELLEMONT CHART A** over 15 sts, pm in chart color, p1, k1tbl, p1, knit to m, M1R, sl m, *k1, M1L, knit to chart m, sl chart m, work 15 chart sts, sl chart m, knit to 1 st before m, M1R, k1,* sl m, M1L, knit across back sts to next m, M1R, sl m; rep from * to * for right sleeve, sl m, M1L, knit to 3 sts before chart m, p1, k1tbl, p1, sl chart m, work Row 1 of **BELLEMONT CHART B** over 15 sts, sl chart m, k2—249 sts; 37 sts each front, 73 back sts, 51 sleeve sts.

note: *The front and sleeve lace patterns may be on different chart rows; keep track of the patterns separately if necessary.*

ROW 40: Sl 1, work in established patts to end of row.

ROW 41: (body only inc row) Sl 1, k1, sl chart m, work 15 chart sts, sl chart m, p1, k1tbl, p1, knit to m, M1R, sl m, *knit to chart m, sl chart m, work 15 chart sts, sl chart m, knit to next m,* sl m, M1L, knit across back sts to next m, M1R, sl m; rep from * to * for right sleeve, sl m, M1L, knit to 3 sts before chart m, p1, k1tbl, p1, sl chart m, work 15 chart sts, sl chart m, k2—4 sts inc'd; 1 st each front, 2 back sts, no change to sleeve st count.

ROW 42: Sl 1, work in established patts to end of row.

ROW 43: (body and sleeve inc row) Sl 1, k1, sl chart m, work 15 chart sts, sl chart m, p1, k1tbl, p1, knit to m, M1R, sl m, *k1, M1L, knit to chart m, sl chart m, work 15 chart sts, sl chart m, knit to 1 st before m, M1R, k1,* sl m, M1L, knit across back sts to next m, M1R, sl m; rep from * to * for right sleeve, sl m, M1L, knit to 3 sts before chart m, p1, k1tbl, p1, sl chart m, work 15 chart sts, sl chart m, k2—8 sts inc'd; 1 st each front, 2 sts each for back and sleeves.

ROW 44: Sl 1, work in established patts to end of row.

ROWS 45-48: Rep Rows 41–44 once more—273 sts; 41 sts each front, 81 back sts, 55 sleeve sts.

ROWS 49 AND 50: Work 2 rows even as established, without increasing on RS Row 49.

ROW 51: (body and sleeve inc row) Rep Row 43—8 sts inc'd; 1 st each front, 2 sts each for back and sleeves.

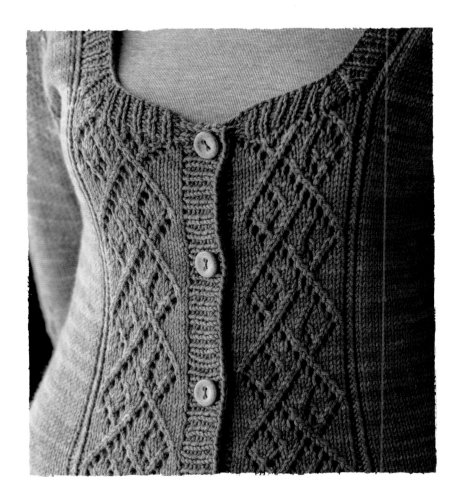

ROW 52: Sl 1, work in established patts to end of row.

ROWS 53-56: Rep Rows 49–52 once more—289 sts; 43 sts each front, 85 back sts, 59 sleeve sts; yoke measures 8" (20.5 cm) from CO.

Make a note of the last chart row completed on the sleeves so you can resume working them with the correct row later.

SIZE 40½" ONLY

ROW 1: (RS) Sl 1, M1R (see Glossary), slip raglan marker (sl m), k1, M1L (see Glossary), sl chart m, work Row 1 of **BELLEMONT CHART B** over center 15 left sleeve sts, sl chart m, M1R, k1, sl m, M1L, knit across back sts to next m, M1R, sl m, k1, M1L, sl chart m, work Row 1 of **BELLEMONT CHART A** over center 15 right sleeve sts, sl chart m, M1R, k1, sl m, M1L, k1—8 sts inc'd; 1 st each front, 2 sts each for back and sleeves.

ROW 2: (WS) Sl 1, work in established patts, purling the last st and working new sts in St st.

ROW 3: Sl 1, p1, M1R, sl m, *k1, M1L, knit to chart m, sl chart m, work 15 chart sts, sl chart m, knit to 1 st before m, M1R, k1.* sl m, M1L, knit across back sts to next m, M1R, sl m; rep from * to * for right sleeve, sl m, M1L, p1, k1—89 sts; 3 sts each front, 41 back sts, 21 sleeve sts.

ROW 4: Sl 1, work in established patts to end of row.

ROW 5: (body and sleeve inc row) Sl 1, p1, knit to m, M1R, sl m, *k1, M1L, knit to chart m, sl chart m, work 15 chart sts, sl chart m, knit to 1 st before m, M1R, k1,* sl m, M1L, knit across back sts to next m, M1R, sl m; rep from * to * for right sleeve, sl m, M1L, knit to last 2 sts, p1, k1—8 sts inc'd; 1 st each front, 2 sts each for back and sleeves.

ROW 6: Sl 1, work in established patts to end of row.

ROWS 7–31: Rep Rows 5 and 6 twelve more times, then work Row 5 once more—201 sts; 17 sts each front, 69 back sts, 49 sleeve sts.

ROW 32: Sl 1, work in established patts to end of row.

ROW 33: (body only inc row) Sl 1, p1, knit to m, M1R, sl m, *knit to chart m, sl chart m, work 15 chart sts, sl chart m, knit to next m,* sl m, M1L, knit across back sts to next m, M1R, sl m; rep from * to * for right sleeve, sl m, M1L, knit to last 2 sts, p1, k1—4 sts inc'd; 1 st each front, 2 back sts, no change to sleeve st count.

ROW 34: Sl 1, work in established patts to end of row.

ROW 35: (body and sleeve inc row) Rep Row 5—8 sts inc'd; 1 st each front, 2 sts each for back and sleeves.

ROW 36: Sl 1, work in established patts to end of row.

ROWS 37–40: Rep Rows 33–36 once more—225 sts; 21 sts each front, 77 back sts, 53 sleeve sts.

ROW 41: (body only inc row) Rep Row 33—229 sts; 22 sts each front, 79 back sts, 53 sleeve sts; yoke measures about 6" (15 cm) from CO.

ROW 42: (WS) Use the backward-loop method (see Glossary) to CO 18 sts for right front neck. Beg by working across newly CO sts, p2, pm in chart color, p15, pm in chart color, k1, p1 through the back loop (tbl), k1, work in established patts to last 2 sts, k1, p1, then use the backward-loop method to CO 18 sts for left front neck—40 sts each front.

ROW 43: (body and sleeve inc row) Beg by working across newly CO sts, sl 1, k1, pm in chart color, work Row 1 of **BELLEMONT CHART A** over 15 sts, pm in chart color, p1, k1tbl, p1, knit to m, M1R, sl m, *k1, M1L, knit to chart m, sl chart m, work 15 chart sts, sl chart m, knit to 1 st before m, M1R, k1,* sl m, M1L, knit across back sts to next m, M1R, sl m; rep from * to * for right sleeve, sl m, M1L, knit to 3 sts before chart m, p1, k1tbl, p1, sl chart m, work Row 1 of **BELLEMONT CHART B** over 15 sts, sl chart m, k2—273 sts; 41 sts each front, 81 back sts, 55 sleeve sts.

note: *The front and sleeve lace patterns may be on different chart rows; keep track of the patterns separately if necessary.*

ROW 44: Sl 1, work in established patts.

ROW 45: (body only inc row) Sl 1, k1, sl chart m, work 15 chart sts, sl chart m, p1, k1tbl, p1, knit to m, M1R, sl m, *knit to chart m, sl chart m, work 15 chart sts, sl chart m, knit to next m,* sl m, M1L, knit across back sts to next m, M1R, sl m; rep from * to * for right sleeve, sl m, M1L, knit to 3 sts before chart m, p1, k1tbl, p1, sl chart m, work 15 chart sts, sl chart m, k2—4 sts inc'd; 1 st each front, 2 back sts, no change to sleeve st count.

ROW 46: Sl 1, work in established patts to end of row.

ROW 47: (body and sleeve inc row) Sl 1, k1, sl chart m, work 15 chart sts, sl chart m, p1, k1tbl, p1, knit to m, M1R, sl m, *k1, M1L, knit to chart m, sl chart m, work 15 chart sts, sl chart m, knit to 1 st before m, M1R, k1,* sl m, M1L, knit across back sts to next m, M1R, sl m; rep from * to * for right sleeve, sl m, M1L, knit to 3 sts before chart m, p1, k1tbl, p1, sl chart m, work 15 chart sts, sl chart m, k2—8 sts inc'd; 1 st each front, 2 sts each for back and sleeves.

ROW 48: Sl 1, work in established patts to end of row.

ROWS 49–56: Rep Rows 45–48 two more times—309 sts; 47 sts each front, 93 back sts, 61 sleeve sts.

ROWS 57 AND 58: Work 2 rows even as established, without increasing on RS Row 57.

ROW 59: (body and sleeve inc row) Rep Row 47—317 sts; 48 sts each front, 95 back sts, 63 sleeve sts.

ROW 60: Sl 1, work in established patts—yoke measures 8½" (21.5 cm) from CO.

Make a note of the last chart row completed on the sleeves so you can resume working them with the correct row later.

SIZE 44½" ONLY

ROW 1: (RS) Sl 1, M1R (see Glossary), slip raglan marker (sl m), k1, M1L (see Glossary), sl chart m, work Row 1 of **BELLEMONT CHART B** over center 15 left sleeve sts, sl chart m, M1R, k1, sl m, M1L, knit across back sts to next m, M1R, sl m, k1, M1L, sl chart m, work Row 1 of **BELLEMONT CHART A** over center 15 right sleeve sts, sl chart m, M1R, k1, sl m, M1L, k1—8 sts inc'd; 1 st each front, 2 sts each for back and sleeves.

ROW 2: (WS) Sl 1, work in established patts, purling the last st and working new sts in St st.

ROW 3: (body and sleeve inc row) Sl 1, knit to m, M1R, sl m, *k1, M1L, knit to chart m, sl chart m, work 15 chart sts, sl chart m, knit to 1 st before m, M1R, k1,* sl m, M1L, knit across back sts to next m, M1R, sl m; rep from * to * for right sleeve, sl m, M1L, knit to end—8 sts inc'd; 1 st each front, 2 sts each for back and sleeves.

ROW 4: Sl 1, work in established patts to end of row.

ROWS 5–45: Rep Rows 3 and 4 twenty more times, then work Row 3 once more—263 sts; 24 sts each front, 89 back sts, 63 sleeve sts; yoke measures about 6½" (16.5 cm) from CO.

ROW 46: (WS) Use the backward-loop method (see Glossary) to CO 21 sts for right front neck. Beg by working across newly CO sts, p2, pm in chart color, p15, pm in chart color, k1, p1tbl, k1, p1, work in established patts to end, then use the backward-loop method to CO 21 sts for left front neck—45 sts each front.

ROW 47: (body and sleeve inc row) Beg by working across newly CO sts, sl 1, k1, pm in chart color, work Row 1 of **BELLEMONT CHART A** over 15 sts, pm in chart color, p1, k1tbl, p1, knit to m, M1R, sl m, *k1, M1L, knit to chart m, sl chart m, work 15 chart sts, sl chart m, knit to 1 st before m, M1R, k1,* sl m, M1L, knit across back sts to next m, M1R, sl m; rep from * to * for right sleeve, sl m, M1L, knit to 3 sts before chart m, p1, k1tbl, p1, sl chart m, work Row 1 of **BELLEMONT CHART B** over 15 sts, sl chart m, k2—313 sts; 46 sts each front, 91 back sts, 65 sleeve sts.

note: *The front and sleeve lace patterns may be on different chart rows; keep track of the patterns separately if necessary.*

ROW 48: Sl 1, work in established patts to end of row.

ROW 49: (body only inc row) Sl 1, k1, sl chart m, work 15 chart sts, sl chart m, p1, k1tbl, p1, knit to m, M1R, sl m, *knit to chart m, sl chart m, work 15 chart sts, sl chart m, knit to m,* sl m, M1L, knit across back sts to next m, M1R, sl m; rep from * to * for right sleeve, sl m, M1L, knit to 3 sts before chart m, p1, k1tbl, p1, sl chart m, work 15 chart sts, sl chart m, k2—4 sts inc'd; 1 st each front, 2 back sts, no change to sleeve st count.

ROW 50: Sl 1, work in established patts to end of row.

ROW 51: (body and sleeve inc row) Sl 1, k1, sl chart m, work 15 chart sts, sl chart m, p1, k1tbl, p1, knit to m, M1R, sl m, *k1, M1L, knit to chart m, sl chart m, work 15 chart sts, sl chart m, knit to 1 st before m, M1R, k1,* sl m, M1L, knit across back sts to next m, M1R, sl m; rep from * to * for right sleeve, sl m, M1L, knit to 3 sts before chart m, p1, k1tbl, p1, sl chart m, work 15 chart sts, sl chart m, k2—8 sts inc'd; 1 st each front, 2 sts each for back and sleeves.

ROW 52: Sl 1, work in established patts to end of row.

ROWS 53–60: Rep Rows 49–52 two more times—349 sts; 52 sts each front, 103 back sts, 71 sleeve sts.

ROWS 61 AND 62: Work 2 rows even as established, without inc on RS Row 61.

ROW 63: (body and sleeve inc row) Rep Row 51—357 sts; 53 sts each front, 105 back sts, 73 sleeve sts.

ROW 64: Sl 1, work in established patts—yoke measures 9¼" (23.5 cm) from CO.

Make a note of the last chart row completed on the sleeves so you can resume working them with the correct row later.

SIZE 48½" ONLY

ROW 1: (RS) Sl 1, M1R (see Glossary), slip raglan marker (sl m), k1, M1L (see Glossary), knit to chart m, sl chart m, work Row 1 of **BELLEMONT CHART B** over center 15 left sleeve sts, sl chart m, knit to 1 st before next m, M1R, k1, sl m, M1L, knit across back sts to next m, M1R, sl m, k1, M1L, knit to chart m, sl chart m, work Row 1 of **BELLEMONT CHART A** over center 15 right sleeve sts, sl chart m, knit to 1 st before next m, M1R, k1, sl m, M1L, k1—8 sts inc'd; 1 st each front, 2 sts each for back and sleeves.

ROW 2: (WS) Sl 1, work in established patts, purling the last st and working new sts in St st.

ROW 3: (body and sleeve inc row) Sl 1, knit to m, M1R, sl m, *k1, M1L, knit to chart m, sl chart m, work 15 chart sts, sl chart m, knit to 1 st before m, M1R, k1,* sl m, M1L, knit across back sts to next m, M1R, sl m; rep from * to * for right sleeve, sl m, M1L, knit to end—8 sts inc'd; 1 st each front, 2 sts each for back and sleeves.

ROW 4: Sl 1, work in established patts to end of row.

ROWS 5–47: Rep Rows 3 and 4 twenty-one more times, then work Row 3 once more—279 sts; 25 sts each front, 95 back sts, 67 sleeve sts; yoke measures about 7" (18 cm) from CO.

ROW 48: (WS) Use the backward-loop method (see Glossary) to CO 23 sts for right front neck. Beg by working across newly CO sts, p2, pm in chart color, p15, pm in chart color, k1, p1 through the back loop (tbl), k1, p3, work in established patts to end, then use the backward-loop method to CO 23 sts for left front neck—48 sts each front.

ROW 49: (body and sleeve inc row) Beg by working across newly CO sts, sl 1, k1, pm in chart color, work Row 1 of **BELLEMONT CHART A** over 15 sts, pm in chart color, p1, k1tbl, p1, knit to m, M1R, sl m, *k1, M1L, knit to chart m, sl chart m, work 15 chart sts, sl chart m, knit to 1 st before m, M1R, k1,* sl m, M1L, knit across back sts to next m, M1R, sl m; rep from * to * for right sleeve, sl m, M1L, knit to 3 sts before chart m, p1, k1tbl, p1, sl chart m, work Row 1 of **BELLEMONT CHART B** over 15 sts, sl chart m, k2—333 sts; 49 sts each front, 97 back sts, 69 sleeve sts.

note: *The front and sleeve lace patterns may be on different chart rows; keep track of the patterns separately if necessary.*

ROW 50: Sl 1, work in established patts to end of row.

ROW 51: (body and sleeve inc row) Sl 1, k1, sl chart m, work 15 chart sts, sl chart m, p1, k1tbl, p1, knit to m, M1R, sl m, *k1, M1L, knit to chart m, sl chart m, work 15 chart sts, sl chart m, knit to 1 st before m, M1R, k1,* sl m, M1L, knit across back sts to next m, M1R, sl m; rep from * to

* for right sleeve, sl m, M1L, knit to 3 sts before chart m, p1, k1tbl, p1, sl chart m, work 15 chart sts, sl chart m, k2—8 sts inc'd; 1 st each front, 2 sts each for back and sleeves.

ROW 52: Sl 1, work in established patts to end of row.

ROWS 53-60: Rep Rows 51 and 52 four more times—373 sts; 54 sts each front, 107 back sts, 79 sleeve sts.

ROW 61: (body only inc row) Sl 1, k1, sl chart m, work 15 chart sts, sl chart m, p1, k1tbl, p1, knit to m, M1R, sl m, *knit to chart m, sl chart m, work 15 chart sts, sl chart m, knit to m,* sl m, M1L, knit across back sts to next m, M1R, sl m; rep from * to * for right sleeve, sl m, M1L, knit to 3 sts

before chart m, p1, k1tbl, p1, sl chart m, work 15 chart sts, sl chart m, k2—4 sts inc'd; 1 st each front, 2 back sts, no change to sleeve st count.

ROW 62: Sl 1, work in established patts to end of row.

ROW 63: (body and sleeve inc row) Rep Row 51—8 sts inc'd; 1 st each front, 2 sts each for back and sleeves.

ROW 64: Sl 1, work in established patts to end of row.

ROWS 65-68: Rep Rows 61–64 once more—397 sts; 58 sts each front, 115 back sts, 83 sleeve sts; yoke measures 9¾" (25 cm) from CO.

Make a note of the last chart row completed on the sleeves so you can resume working them with the correct row later.

SIZES (52½, 56½)" ONLY

ROW 1: (RS) Sl 1, M1R (see Glossary), slip raglan marker (sl m), k1, M1L (see Glossary), knit to chart m, sl chart m, work Row 1 of **BELLEMONT CHART B** over center 15 left sleeve sts, sl chart m, knit to 1 st before next m, M1R, k1, sl m, M1L, knit across back sts to next m, M1R, sl m, k1, M1L, knit to chart m, sl chart m, work Row 1 of **BELLEMONT CHART A** over center 15 right sleeve sts, sl chart m, knit to 1 st before next m, M1R, k1, sl m, M1L, k1—8 sts inc'd; 1 st each front, 2 sts each for back and sleeves.

ROW 2: (WS) Sl 1, work in established patts, purling the last st and working new sts in St st.

ROW 3: (body and sleeve inc row) Sl 1, knit to m, M1R, sl m, *k1, M1L, knit to chart m, sl chart m, work 15 chart sts, sl chart m, knit to 1 st before m, M1R, k1,* sl m, M1L, knit across back sts to next m, M1R, sl m; rep from * to * for right sleeve, sl m, M1L, knit to end—8 sts inc'd; 1 st each front, 2 sts each for back and sleeves.

ROW 4: Sl 1, work in established patts to end of row.

ROW 5 TO ROW (49, 53): Rep the last 2 rows (22, 24) more times, then work Row 3 once more—(303, 329) sts; (26, 28) sts each front, (105, 115) back sts, (73, 79) sleeve sts; yoke measures about (7¼, 7¾)" (18.5 [19.5] cm) from CO.

ROW (50, 54): (WS) Use the backward-loop method (see Glossary) to CO (27, 30) sts for right front neck. Beg by working across newly CO sts, p2, pm in chart color, p15, pm in chart color, k1, p1 through the back loop (tbl), k1, p(7, 10), work in established patts to end, then use the backward-loop method to CO (27, 30) sts for left front neck—(53, 58) sts each front.

ROW (51, 55): (RS) Beg by working across newly CO sts, sl 1, k1, pm in chart color, work Row 1 of **BELLEMONT CHART A** over 15 sts, pm in chart color, p1, k1tbl, p1, knit to m, M1R, sl m, *k1, M1L, knit to chart m, sl chart m, work 15 chart sts, sl chart m, knit to 1 st before m, M1R, k1,* sl m, M1L, knit across back sts to next m, M1R, sl m; rep from * to * for right sleeve, sl m, M1L, knit to 3 sts before chart m, p1, k1tbl, p1, sl chart m, work Row 1 of **BELLEMONT CHART B** over 15 sts, sl chart m, k2—(365, 397) sts; (54, 59) sts each front, (107, 117) back sts, (75, 81) sleeve sts.

note: *The front and sleeve lace patterns may be on different chart rows; keep track of the patterns separately if necessary.*

ROW (52, 56): Sl 1, work in established patts to end of row.

ROW (53, 57): (body and sleeve inc row) Sl 1, k1, sl chart m, work 15 chart sts, sl chart m, p1, k1tbl, p1, knit to m, M1R, sl m, *k1, M1L, knit to chart m, sl chart m, work 15 chart sts, sl chart m, knit to 1 st before m, M1R, k1,* sl m, M1L, knit across back sts to next m, M1R, sl m; rep from * to * for right sleeve, sl m, M1L, knit to 3 sts before chart m, p1, k1tbl, p1, sl chart m, work 15 chart sts, sl chart m, k2—8 sts inc'd; 1 st each front, 2 sts each for back and sleeves.

ROW (54, 58): Sl 1, work in established patts to end of row.

ROW (55, 59) TO ROW 62: Rep the last 2 rows (4, 2) more times—(405, 421) sts; (59, 62) sts each front, (117, 123) back sts, (85, 87) sleeve sts.

ROW 63: (body only inc row) Sl 1, k1, sl chart m, work 15 chart sts, sl chart m, p1, k1tbl, p1, knit to m, M1R, sl m, *knit to chart m, sl chart m, work 15 chart sts, sl chart m, knit to m,* sl m, M1L, knit across back sts to next m, M1R, sl m; rep from * to * for right sleeve, sl m, M1L, knit to 3 sts before chart m, p1, k1tbl, p1, sl chart m, work 15 chart sts, sl chart m, k2—4 sts inc'd; 1 st each front, 2 back sts, no change to sleeve st count.

ROW 64: Sl 1, work in established patts to end of row.

ROW 65: (body and sleeve inc row) Rep Row (53, 57)—8 sts inc'd; 1 st each front, 2 sts each for back and sleeves.

ROW 66: Sl 1, work in established patts to end of row.

ROW 67 TO ROW (70, 74): Rep Rows 63–66 (one, two) more time(s)—(429, 457) sts; (63, 68) sts each front, (125, 135) back sts, (89, 93) sleeve sts; yoke measures 10 (10½)" (25.5 [26.5] cm) from CO.

Make a note of the last chart row completed on the sleeves so you can resume working them with the correct row later.

DIVIDE BODY AND SLEEVES

NEXT ROW: (RS) Removing raglan m as you come to them and leaving chart m in place, work as established to sleeve m, place next 59 (63, 73, 83, 89, 93) sts onto holder for left sleeve, use the backward-loop method to CO 1 st, pm for left side, CO 2 sts as before, work as established to next sleeve m, place next 59 (63, 73, 83, 89, 93) sts onto holder for right sleeve, use the backward-loop method to CO 2 sts, pm for right side, CO 1 st as before, work as established to end—177 (197, 217, 237, 257, 277) sts total; 44 (49, 54, 59, 64, 69) sts each front, 89 (99, 109, 119, 129, 139) back sts.

lower body

SET-UP ROW: (WS) Work as established to side-seam m, sl m, p1, k1, work as established to 2 sts before side-seam m, k1, p1, sl m, work as established to end.

Keeping the side "seam" sts in Rev st st (purl on RS; knit on WS), work even in established patts until piece measures 1" (2.5 cm) from dividing row, ending with a WS row.

SHAPE WAIST

DEC ROW: (RS) Keeping in established patts, work to 2 sts before side-seam m, ssk, sl m, p1, k2tog, work to 3 sts before side-seam m, ssk, p1, sl m, k2tog, work to end—4 sts dec'd, 1 st each front, 2 back sts.

Work 17 rows even, then rep the dec row—169 (189, 209, 229, 249, 269) sts rem.

[Work 15 rows even, then rep the dec row] 2 times—161 (181, 201, 221, 241, 261) sts rem; 40 (45, 50, 55, 60, 65) sts each front, 81 (91, 101, 111, 121, 131) back sts; piece measures 8¼" (21 cm) from dividing row.

Work even as established for 1" (2.5 cm).

INC ROW: (RS) Keeping in established patts, work to side seam m, M1R, sl m, p1, M1L, work to 1 st before side seam m, M1R, p1, sl m, M1L, work to end—4 sts inc'd; 1 st each front, 2 back sts.

Working new sts in st st, work 15 rows even, then rep the inc row—169 (189, 209, 229, 249, 269) sts.

[Work 17 rows even, and then rep the inc row] 2 times—177 (197, 217, 237, 257, 277) sts; 44 (49, 54, 59, 64, 69) sts each front, 89 (99, 109, 119, 129, 139) back sts; piece measures 16¾" (42.5 cm): from dividing row.

Work even if necessary for your size until piece measures about 16¾ (16¾, 16¾, 17, 17, 17¼)" (42.5 [42.5, 42.5, 43, 43, 44] cm) from dividing row, ending with a WS row.

PICOT HEM

Change to working all sts in St st, and work 6 rows even, ending with a WS row—piece measures about 17¾ (17¾, 17¾, 18, 18, 18¼)" (45 [45, 45, 45.5, 45.5, 46.5] cm) from dividing row.

PICOT ROW: (RS) *K2tog, yo; rep from * to last 3 sts, k3tog—175 (195, 215, 235, 255, 275) sts.

Work in St st for 5 rows for hem facing, beg and ending with a WS row.

BO all sts.

sleeves

note: *Resume working lace patt for sleeve with the next odd-numbered chart row of the established patt. Work chart patt in the rnd, working the even-numbered chart rows as knit rnds.*

Distribute 59 (63, 73, 83, 89, 93) held sleeve sts as evenly as possible on 3 or 4 dpn. Join yarn with RS facing at center of underarm, pick up and knit 2 sts, work sleeve sts in established patt, resuming lace patt with the correct chart row, pick up and knit 1 st, pm for beg of rnd—62 (66, 76, 86, 92, 96) sts total.

Join for working in rnds, and work all foll chart rows as RS rnds.

SET-UP RND: P1, work in established patts to end of rnd.

Cont in established patts until piece measures 1" (2.5 cm) from pick-up rnd.

DEC RND: P1, k2tog, work as established to last 2 sts, ssk—2 sts dec'd.

[Work 13 (13, 9, 7, 7, 7) rnds even, then rep the dec rnd] 6 (2, 9, 9, 3, 3) times—48 (60, 56, 66, 84, 88) sts rem.

[Work 11 (11, 7, 5, 5, 5) rnds even, then rep the dec rnd] 2 (7, 3, 7, 15, 15) times—44 (46, 50, 52, 54, 58) sts rem; piece measures 16½ (17¼, 17½, 17½, 17½, 17½)" (42 [44, 44.5, 44.5, 44.5, 44.5] cm) from underarm.

PICOT HEM

Knit 6 rnds.

PICOT RND: *K2tog, yo; rep from *— piece measures 17½ (18¼, 18½, 18½, 18½, 18½)" (44.5 [45.6, 47, 47, 47, 47] cm) from underarm.

Knit 5 rnds for hem facing.

BO all sts.

finishing

Block to measurements. Fold lower body and cuff hems to WS along picot row or rnd and use whipstitch (see Glossary) to tack the BO edge of each hem in place.

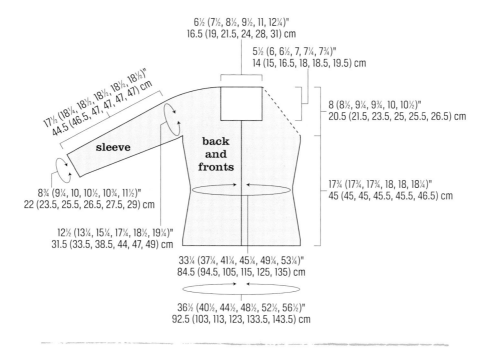

6½ (7½, 8½, 9½, 11, 12¼)"
16.5 (19, 21.5, 24, 28, 31) cm

5½ (6, 6½, 7, 7¼, 7¾)"
14 (15, 16.5, 18, 18.5, 19.5) cm

17½ (18¼, 18½, 18½, 18½, 18½)"
44.5 (46.5, 47, 47, 47, 47) cm

8 (8½, 9¼, 9¾, 10, 10½)"
20.5 (21.5, 23.5, 25, 25.5, 26.5) cm

sleeve

back and fronts

8¾ (9¼, 10, 10½, 10¾, 11½)"
22 (23.5, 25.5, 26.5, 27.5, 29) cm

17¾ (17¾, 17¾, 18, 18, 18¼)"
45 (45, 45, 45.5, 45.5, 46.5) cm

12½ (13¼, 15¼, 17¼, 18½, 19¼)"
31.5 (33.5, 38.5, 44, 47, 49) cm

33¼ (37¼, 41¼, 45¼, 49¼, 53¼)"
84.5 (94.5, 105, 115, 125, 135) cm

36½ (40½, 44½, 48½, 52½, 56½)"
92.5 (103, 113, 123, 133.5, 143.5) cm

NECKBAND

With longer cir needle, RS facing, and beg at right front neck edge, pick up and knit 15 (17, 21, 23, 27, 29) right front sts to corner, pm, 1 st in corner, pm, 29 (32, 33, 36, 37, 40) sts along right neck edge, 17 (17, 17, 19, 23, 25) sts across right sleeve, 33 (37, 43, 47, 55, 61) sts across back neck, 17 (17, 17, 19, 23, 25) sts across left sleeve, 29 (32, 33, 36, 37, 40) sts along left neck edge to corner, pm, 1 st in corner, pm, 15 (17, 21, 23, 27, 29) left front sts to left front edge—157 (171, 187, 205, 231, 251) sts total.

NEXT ROW: (WS) [P1, k1] 7 (8, 10, 11, 13, 14) times, p1, sl m, k1 (corner st), sl m, [p1, k1] 62 (67, 71, 78, 87, 95) times, p1, sl m, k1 (corner st), sl m, [p1, k1] 7 (8, 10, 11, 13, 14) times, p1.

DEC ROW: (RS) *Work sts as they appear (knit the knits and purl the purls) to 2 sts before corner st, ssk,

sl m, p1, sl m, k2tog; rep from * once more—4 sts dec'd.

Working sts as they appear, [work 1 row even, then rep the dec row] 2 more times, then work a WS row—145 (159, 175, 193, 219, 239) sts rem; neckband measures 1" (2.5 cm) from pick-up row.

BO all sts in rib patt.

BUTTONBAND

With cir needle, RS facing, and beg at BO edge of neckband, pick up and knit 97 (97, 99, 99, 99, 101) sts evenly spaced along left front edge, picking up through both layers of the hem and ending at the picot row.

SET-UP ROW: (WS) *P1, k1; rep from * to last st, p1.

Work even in established rib patt until band measures 1" (2.5 cm).

BO all sts in patt.

BUTTONHOLE BAND

Mark placement of six buttonholes on right front, the lowest ¾" (2 cm) above lower body picot row, the highest centered on the neckband, and the rem four evenly spaced in between.

With cir needle, RS facing, beg at picot row, and picking up through both layers of the hem, pick up and knit 97 (97, 99, 99, 99, 101) sts evenly spaced along right front edge, ending at the neckband BO edge.

SET-UP ROW: (WS) *P1, k1; rep from * to last st, p1.

Work even in established rib patt until band measures ½" (1.3 cm), ending with a WS row.

BUTTONHOLE ROW: (RS) Keeping in patt, work a 1-st buttonhole (yo, k2tog) opposite each marked buttonhole position.

Work even in established rib patt until band measures 1" (2.5 cm).

BO all sts in patt.

Weave in loose ends. Block again if desired.

Engleside
cowl-neck pullover

Worked top down with raglan shaping, this pullover features a wide cowl neck. The simple stockinette body is jazzed up with zigzag lace on the cowl that is echoed at the bottom hem and sleeve cuffs. I enjoy working top-down sweaters like this because they require minimal finishing and make custom sizing easy. The sweater shown is knitted in a recycled wool yarn with a slight heathered effect that adds visual interest.

finished size
About 30 (33½, 36¾, 41, 44½, 48¾)" (76 [85, 93.5, 104, 113, 124] cm) bust circumference. Sweater shown measures 30" (76 cm).

yarn
DK weight (#3 Light).

Shown here: Universal Yarn Renew Wool (65% virgin wool, 35% repurposed wool; 270 yd [247 m]/100 g): #102 Husk, 4 (5, 6, 6, 7, 7) balls.

Note: This yarn has been discontinued; substitute the DK weight wool or wool-blend yarn of your choice.

needles
Size U.S. 6 (4 mm): 16" (40 cm) and 24" (60 cm) circular (cir) and set of 4 or 5 double-pointed (dpn).

Adjust needle size if necessary to obtain the correct gauge.

notions
Markers (m); tapestry needle.

gauge
23 sts and 30 rnds = 4" (10 cm) in St st, worked in rnds.

NOTES

- This seamless sweater is knitted from the top down in stockinette stitch to the lace lower border and sleeve cuffs.

- Stitches for the cowl neck are picked up from the neck opening and worked in the round.

STITCH GUIDE

ENGLESIDE LACE (multiple of 4 sts)

Rnd 1: *Yo, ssk, k2; rep from *.

Rnd 2: K1, *yo, ssk, k2; rep from * to last 3 sts, yo, ssk, k1.

Rnd 3: K2, *yo, ssk, k2; rep from * to last 2 sts, yo, ssk.

Rnd 4: Remove m, k1 (shaded blue on chart) to transfer first st of rnd to end of rnd, replace m. K2, *yo, ssk, k2; rep from * to last 2 sts, yo, ssk (last st tog with blue-shaded transferred st).

Rnd 5: K1, *k2tog, yo, k2; rep from * to last 3 sts, k2tog, yo, k1.

Rnd 6: *K2tog, yo, k2; rep from *.

Rnd 7: Remove m, k1 (shaded blue on chart) to transfer first st of rnd to end of rnd, replace m. *Yo, k2, k2tog; rep from * to last 4 sts, yo, k2, k2tog (last st tog with blue-shaded transferred st).

Rnd 8: *Yo, k2, k2tog; rep from *.

Rep Rnds 1–8 for patt.

yoke

With shorter cir needle, CO 8 (8, 8, 10, 10, 10) sts for left sleeve, place marker (pm), CO 40 (42, 44, 44, 46, 48) sts for back, pm, CO 8 (8, 8, 10, 10, 10) sts for right sleeve, pm, CO 40 (42, 44, 44, 46, 48) sts for front, pm for beg of rnd—96 (100, 104, 108, 112, 116) sts total; rnd begins at left front raglan at beg of left sleeve sts.

SHAPE YOKE

Change to longer cir needle when there are too many sts to fit around the shorter needle, work according to your size as foll.

SIZE 30" ONLY

RND 1: (body and sleeve inc rnd) *K1 M1L (see Glossary), knit to 1 st before m, M1R (see Glossary), k1, sl m; rep from * 3 more times—8 sts inc'd; 2 sts each for back, front, and each sleeve.

RNDS 2-4: Knit, working new sts in St st.

RNDS 5-16: Rep Rnds 1–4 three more times—128 sts; 48 sts each for back and front; 16 sts each sleeve.

RND 17: (body and sleeve inc rnd) Rep Rnd 1—8 sts inc'd.

RND 18: Knit.

RND 19: (sleeve only inc rnd) *K1 M1L, knit to 1 st before m, M1R, k1, sl m,* knit to end of back sts, sl m; rep from * to * once more for second sleeve, knit to end of front sts—4 sts inc'd; 2 sts each sleeve; no change to back and front.

RND 20: Knit.

RNDS 21-36: Rep Rnds 17–20 four more times—188 sts; 58 sts each for back and front; 36 sts each sleeve.

RND 37: (body and sleeve inc rnd) Rep Rnd 1—8 sts inc'd.

RND 38: Knit.

RNDS 39-58: Rep Rnds 37 and 38 ten more times—276 sts; 80 sts each for back and front; 58 sts each sleeve; yoke measures 7¾" (19.5 cm) from CO.

SIZE 33½" ONLY

RND 1: (body and sleeve inc rnd) *K1 M1L (see Glossary), knit to 1 st before m, M1R (see Glossary), k1, sl m; rep from * 3 more times—8 sts inc'd; 2 sts each for back, front, and each sleeve.

RNDS 2-4: Knit, working new sts in St st.

RNDS 5-12: Rep Rnds 1–4 two more times—124 sts; 48 sts each for back and front; 14 sts each sleeve.

RND 13: (sleeve only inc rnd) *K1 M1L, knit to 1 st before m, M1R, k1, sl m,* knit to end of back sts, sl m; rep from * to * once more for second sleeve, knit to end of front sts—4 sts inc'd; 2 sts each sleeve; no change to back and front.

RND 14: Knit.

RND 15: (body and sleeve inc rnd) Rep Rnd 1—8 sts inc'd.

RND 16: Knit.

RNDS 17-28: Rep Rnds 13–16 three more times—172 sts; 56 sts each for back and front; 30 sts each sleeve.

RND 29: (body and sleeve inc rnd) Rep Rnd 1—8 sts inc'd.

RND 30: Knit.

RNDS 31-62: Rep Rnds 29 and 30 sixteen more times—308 sts; 90 sts each for back and front; 64 sts each sleeve; yoke measures 8¼" (21 cm) from CO.

SIZE 36¾" ONLY

RND 1: (body and sleeve inc rnd) *K1 M1L (see Glossary), knit to 1 st before m, M1R (see Glossary), k1, sl m; rep from * 3 more times—8 sts inc'd; 2 sts each for back, front, and each sleeve.

RNDS 2-4: Knit, working new sts in St st.

RNDS 5-8: Rep Rnds 1–4 once more— 120 sts; 48 sts each for back and front; 12 sts each sleeve.

RND 9: (body and sleeve inc rnd) Rep Rnd 1—8 sts inc'd.

RND 10: Knit.

RND 11: (sleeve only inc rnd) *K1 M1L, knit to 1 st before m, M1R, k1, sl m,* knit to end of back sts, sl m; rep from * to * once more for second sleeve, knit to end of front sts—4 sts inc'd; 2 sts each sleeve; no change to back and front.

RND 12: Knit.

RNDS 13-20: Rep Rnds 9–12 two times—156 sts; 54 sts each for back and front; 24 sts each sleeve.

RND 21: (body and sleeve inc rnd) Rep Rnd 1—8 sts inc'd.

RND 22: Knit.

RNDS 23-66: Rep Rnds 21 and 22 twenty-two times—340 sts; 100 sts each for back and front; 70 sts each sleeve; yoke measures 8¾" (22 cm) from CO.

SIZE 41" ONLY

RND 1: (body and sleeve inc rnd) *K1 M1L (see Glossary), knit to 1 st before m, M1R (see Glossary), k1, sl m; rep from * 3 more times—8 sts inc'd; 2 sts each for back, front, and each sleeve.

RNDS 2-4: Knit, working new sts in St st.

RNDS 5-12: Rep Rnds 1–4 two more times—132 sts; 50 sts each for back and front; 16 sts each sleeve.

RND 13: (body and sleeve inc rnd) Rep Rnd 1—8 sts inc'd.

RND 14: Knit.

RNDS 15-72: Rep Rnds 13 and 14 twenty-nine more times—372 sts; 110 sts each for back and front; 76 sts each sleeve; yoke measures 9½" (24 cm) from CO.

SIZE 44½" ONLY

RND 1: (body and sleeve inc rnd) *K1 M1L (see Glossary), knit to 1 st before m, M1R (see Glossary), k1, sl m; rep from * 3 more times—8 sts inc'd; 2 sts each for back, front, and each sleeve.

RNDS 2-4: Knit, working new sts in St st.

RNDS 5-8: Rep Rnds 1–4 once more—128 sts; 50 sts each for back and front; 14 sts each sleeve.

RND 9: (body and sleeve inc rnd) Rep Rnd 1—8 sts inc'd.

Engleside

					8
					*7
					6
					5
					*4
					3
					2
					1

4-st repeat
*See Stitch Guide

☐ knit
⊡ yo
╱ k2tog
╲ ssk
▨ see Stitch Guide
☐ pattern repeat

RND 10: Knit.

RNDS 11–78: Rep Rnds 9 and 10 thirty-four more times—408 sts; 120 sts each for back and front; 84 sts each sleeve; yoke measures 10½" (26.5 cm) from CO.

SIZE 48¾" ONLY

RND 1: (body and sleeve inc rnd) *K1 M1L (see Glossary), knit to 1 st before m, M1R (see Glossary), k1, sl m; rep from * 3 more times—8 sts inc'd; 2 sts each for back, front, and each sleeve.

RND 2: Knit, working new sts in St st.

RND 3: (body only inc rnd) Knit to end of left sleeve, sl m, *k1, M1L, knit to 1 st before m, M1R, k1, sl m,* knit to end of right sleeve, sl m; rep from * to * for front—4 sts inc'd; 2 sts each for back and front; no change to sleeves.

RND 4: Knit.

RNDS 5–8: Rep Rnds 1–4 once more—140 sts; 56 sts each for back and front; 14 sts each sleeve.

RND 9: (body and sleeve inc rnd) Rep Rnd 1—8 sts inc'd.

RND 10: Knit.

RNDS 11–82: Rep Rnds 9 and 10 thirty-six more times—436 sts; 130 sts each for back and front; 88 sts each sleeve; yoke measures 11" (28 cm) from CO.

DIVIDE BODY AND SLEEVES

Removing existing markers when you come to them and placing new markers as indicated, place 58 (64, 70, 76, 84, 88) sts onto holder for left sleeve, use the backward-loop method (see Glossary) to CO 3 (3, 3, 4, 4, 5) sts, pm for new beg of rnd in center of left underarm, CO 3 (3, 3, 4, 4, 5) more sts as before, k80 (90, 100, 110, 120, 130) back sts, place next 58 (64, 70, 76, 84, 88) sts onto holder for right sleeve, use the backward-loop method to CO 3 (3, 3, 4, 4, 5) sts, pm in center of right underarm, CO 3 (3, 3, 4, 4, 5) more sts, k80 (90, 100, 110, 120) front sts, then knit the first 3 (3, 3, 4, 4, 5) CO sts again to end at new beg-of-rnd m at left side—172 (192, 212, 236, 256, 280) sts total; 86 (96, 106, 118, 128, 140) sts each for back and front; rnd begins at left side at start of back sts.

lower body

Knit 7 rnds even.

DEC RND: *K1, k2tog, knit to 3 sts before m, ssk, k1, sl m; rep from * once more—4 sts dec'd; 2 sts each from back and front.

[Knit 7 (7, 7, 5, 5, 5) rnds, then rep the dec rnd] 2 (4, 4, 7, 7, 4) times—160 (172, 192, 204, 224, 260) sts rem.

[Knit 5 (5, 5, 0, 0, 3) rnds, then rep the dec rnd] 4 (2, 2, 0, 0, 4) times—144 (164, 184, 204, 224, 244) sts rem; 72 (82, 92, 102, 112, 122) sts each for front and back.

Knit 8 rnds even.

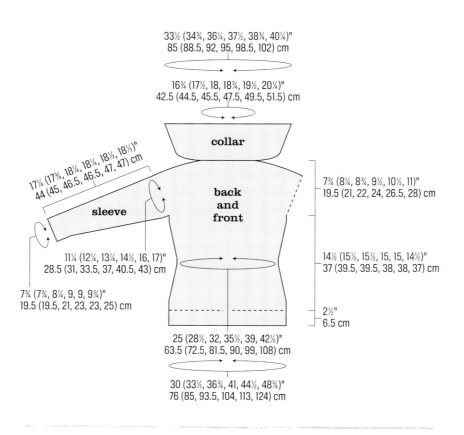

33½ (34¾, 36¼, 37½, 38¾, 40¼)"
85 (88.5, 92, 95, 98.5, 102) cm

16¾ (17½, 18, 18¾, 19½, 20¼)"
42.5 (44.5, 45.5, 47.5, 49.5, 51.5) cm

collar

17¼ (17¾, 18¼, 18¼, 18½, 18½)"
44 (45, 46.5, 46.5, 47, 47) cm

sleeve

back and front

7¾ (8¼, 8¾, 9½, 10½, 11)"
19.5 (21, 22, 24, 26.5, 28) cm

11¼ (12¼, 13¼, 14½, 16, 17)"
28.5 (31, 33.5, 37, 40.5, 43) cm

14½ (15½, 15½, 15, 15, 14½)"
37 (39.5, 39.5, 38, 38, 37) cm

7¾ (7¾, 8¼, 9, 9, 9¾)"
19.5 (19.5, 21, 23, 23, 25) cm

2½"
6.5 cm

25 (28½, 32, 35½, 39, 42½)"
63.5 (72.5, 81.5, 90, 99, 108) cm

30 (33½, 36¾, 41, 44½, 48¾)"
76 (85, 93.5, 104, 113, 124) cm

INC RND: *K1, M1L, knit to 1 st before m, M1R, k1, sl m; rep from * once—4 sts inc'd; 2 sts each for front and back.

[Knit 5 (5, 5, 0, 0, 3) rnds, then rep the inc rnd] 4 (2, 2, 0, 0, 4) times—164 (176, 196, 208, 228, 264) sts.

[Knit 7 (7, 7, 5, 5, 5) rnds, then rep the inc rnd] 2 (4, 4, 7, 7, 4) times—172 (192, 212, 236, 256, 280) sts; 86 (96, 106, 118, 128, 140) sts each for front and back; lower body measures 13 (14, 14, 13½, 13½, 13)" (33 [35.5, 35.5, 34.5, 34.5, 33] cm) from dividing rnd.

Work even in St st until lower body measures 14½ (15½, 15½, 15, 15, 14½)" (37 [39.5, 39.5, 38, 38, 37] cm).

Work Rnds 1–8 of **ENGLESIDE CHART** (see page 119 or Stitch Guide

on page 116) 2 times, then work Rnds 1–4 once more—20 chart rnds completed.

[Purl 1 rnd, knit 1 rnd] 2 times—2 garter ridges completed; lower body measures about 17 (18, 18, 17½, 17½, 17)" (43 [45.5, 45.5, 44.5, 44.5, 43] cm).

note: *The larger sizes have deeper yokes, so their lower bodies are shorter to prevent the overall garment length from becoming too long.*

Loosely BO all sts.

sleeves

Divide 58 (64, 70, 76, 84, 88) held sleeve sts as evenly as possible on 3 or 4 dpn. With RS facing and beg at center of underarm, pick up and knit

3 (3, 3, 4, 4, 5) sts, k58 (64, 70, 76, 84, 88) sleeve sts, pick up and knit 3 (3, 3, 4, 4, 5) sts, pm for beg of rnd—64 (70, 76, 84, 92, 98) sts total.

Knit 8 rnds even.

DEC RND: K1, k2tog, knit to last 3 sts, ssk, k1—2 sts dec'd.

[Knit 11 (0, 7, 7, 5, 5) rnds, then rep the dec rnd] 2 (0, 11, 5, 13, 11) times—58 (68, 52, 72, 64, 74) sts rem.

[Knit 9 (7, 5, 5, 3, 3) rnds, then rep the dec rnd] 7 (12, 2, 10, 6, 9) times—44 (44, 48, 52, 52, 56) sts rem.

Work even until sleeve measures 14¾ (15¼, 15¾, 15¾, 16, 16)" (37.5 [38.5, 40, 40, 40.5, 40.5] cm).

Work Rnds 1–8 of Engleside patt 2 times, then work Rnds 1–4 once more—20 chart rnds completed.

[Purl 1 rnd, knit 1 rnd] 2 times— 2 garter ridges completed; sleeve measures about 17¼ (17¾, 18¼, 18¼, 18½, 18½)" (44 [45, 46.5, 46.5, 47, 47] cm) from pick-up rnd.

Loosely BO all sts.

collar

note: *The RS of the collar corresponds to the WS of the body so the RS of the collar's lace pattern will show on the outside when the collar is folded down; turn garment inside-out to make working the collar easier.*

With shorter cir needle, WS of garment facing, and beg at center back neck, pick up and knit 96 (100, 104, 108, 112, 116) sts evenly spaced around neck opening (1 st for every CO st). Pm and join for working in rnds.

Knit 1 rnd.

NEXT RND: *Yo, k1; rep from *—192 (200, 208, 216, 224, 232) sts.

Knit 1 rnd.

Work Rnds 1–8 of Engleside patt 5 times, then work Rnds 1–4 once more—44 chart rnds completed.

[Purl 1 rnd, knit 1 rnd] 2 times— 2 garter ridges completed; collar measures about 6" (15 cm) from pick-up rnd.

Loosely BO all sts.

finishing

Block to measurements. Weave in loose ends.

Manheim
fitted pullover

This fitted pullover features an allover lace pattern and V-neck shaping. Maintaining the proper stitch count during shaping will test your lace-knitting prowess, but the result is well worth the effort! The pullover is worked from the bottom up in four pieces that are seamed together. Ribbed edges and set-in sleeves keep the look classic and casual. The lightweight and lofty yarn prevents the lace from stretching out of shape.

finished size
About 28 (31½, 35, 38½, 42, 45½, 49)" (71 [80, 89, 98, 106.5, 115.5, 124.5] cm) bust circumference.

Sweater shown measures 31½" (80 cm).

yarn
Sportweight (#2 Fine).

Shown here: Imperial Yarn Tracie Too (100% wool; 395 yd [361 m]/4 oz [113 g]): #351 Autumn Rust, 2 (2, 3, 3, 3, 3, 4) balls.

needles
Size U.S. 5 (3.75 mm): 16" (40 cm) and 24" (60 cm) circular (cir).

Adjust needle size if necessary to obtain the correct gauge.

notions
Markers (m); tapestry needle.

gauge
40 sts (4 patt reps from chart Rows 3–12; see Notes) measure about 7" (18 cm) wide; 60 rows (5 patt reps) measure about 7" (18 cm) high in lace patt from Manheim chart.

NOTES

— For Rows 1 and 2, the Manheim chart temporarily increases from a multiple of 10 stitches plus 1 to a multiple of 13 stitches plus 1, then decreases back to the original 10 stitches plus 1 again for Rows 3–12. If possible, count stitches after completing a row when the normal 10-stitch repeat has been restored. The counts given in the instructions assume this 10-stitch repeat.

— During shaping, be sure to maintain the proper stitch count by working each decrease with its corresponding yarnover, or each double decrease with both its companion yarnovers. If this is not possible, work the stitches in stockinette instead.

STITCH GUIDE
5-INTO-1 DEC

Sl 2 sts as if to k2tog, k1, p2sso, return dec st on right needle to left needle, pass the second and third sts on left needle over the dec st, then sl the dec st to the right needle again—4 sts dec'd; 1 st made from 5 sts.

back

With longer cir needle, CO 106 (118, 130, 142, 154, 166, 178) sts.

SET-UP ROW: (WS) *P2, k2; rep from * to last 2 sts, p2.

Slipping the first st of every row, work in established rib until piece measures 1" (2.5 cm) from CO, ending with a RS row.

NEXT ROW: (WS) Sl 1, purl to end and *at the same time* dec 21 (23, 25, 27, 29, 31, 33) sts evenly spaced—85 (95, 105, 115, 125, 135, 145) sts rem.

NEXT ROW: (RS) Sl 1, k1, work Row 1 of **MANHEIM CHART** to the last 2 sts, k2.

NEXT ROW: Sl 1, p1, work Row 2 of chart to last 2 sts, p2.

Working 2 edge sts at each side as established, work rem sts in chart patt until piece measures 2 (2, 2½, 2½, 3, 3, 3)" (5 [5, 6.5, 6.5, 7.5, 7.5, 7.5] cm) from CO, ending with a WS row.

SHAPE WAIST

DEC ROW: (RS) Sl 1, k1, ssk, work in patt to last 4 sts, k2tog, k2—2 sts dec'd.

[Work 5 rows even in patt, then rep the dec row] 2 (3, 3, 4, 4, 2, 3) times (see Notes)—79 (87, 97, 105, 115, 129, 137) sts rem.

[Work 3 rows even, then rep the dec row] 4 (3, 3, 2, 2, 4, 3) times—71 (81, 91, 101, 111, 121, 131) sts rem; piece measures about 5½ (5¾, 6¼, 6½, 7, 6½, 6¾)" (14 [14.5, 16, 16.5, 18, 16.5, 17] cm) from CO.

Work even as established for 1" (2.5 cm), ending with a WS row.

Manheim

(lace chart, rows 1–11)

multiple of 10 sts + 1, temporarily inc'd to
multiple of 13 sts + 1 for Rows 1 and 2

Legend:

- ☐ knit on RS rows; purl on WS rows
- ◯ yo
- ╱ k2tog
- ╲ ssk
- ↗ k3tog
- ↘ sssk
- ⅄ sl 1, k2tog, psso
- ⑤ 5-into-1 dec (see Stitch Guide)
- ▨ no stitch
- ☐ pattern repeat
- ⌵ k1f&b

INC ROW: (RS) Sl 1, k1, M1L (see Glossary), work in patt to last 2 sts, M1R (see Glossary), k2—2 sts inc'd.

Working new sts into established lace patt, [work 13 rows even, then rep the inc row] 3 (4, 2, 1, 0, 3, 2) time(s)—79 (91, 97, 105, 113, 129, 137) sts.

[Work 11 rows even, then rep the inc row] 1 (0, 2, 3, 4, 1, 2) time(s)—81 (91, 101, 111, 121, 131, 141) sts.

Work even as established for 1" (2.5 cm) more, ending with a WS row—piece measures 14 (14½, 14½, 14½, 14¾, 15, 15)" (35.5 [37, 37, 37, 37.5, 38, 38] cm) from CO.

SHAPE ARMHOLES

Keeping in patt, BO 3 (4, 5, 6, 6, 7, 7) sts at the beg of the next 2 rows—75 (83, 91, 99, 109, 117, 127) sts rem.

BO 3 sts at the beg of the next 2 rows, then BO 2 sts at the beg of the foll 0 (2, 2, 2, 4, 6, 8) rows—69 (73, 81, 89, 95, 99, 105) sts rem.

Dec 1 st at the beg of the next 1 (1, 4, 7, 9, 10, 12) rows—67 (71, 73, 75, 77, 79, 81) sts rem.

Work even in patt until armholes measure 5½ (6, 6½, 7, 7, 7½, 7½)" (14 [15, 16.5, 18, 18, 19, 19] cm), ending with a WS row.

SHAPE NECK AND SHOULDERS

note: *The neck and shoulders are shaped at the same time; read all the way through the next section before proceeding.*

NEXT ROW: (RS) Work 19 (19, 19, 19, 20, 20, 20) sts in patt, join a second ball of yarn, BO center 29 (33, 35, 37, 37, 39, 41) sts, work in patt to end—19 (19, 19, 19, 20, 20, 20) sts rem each side.

Working each side separately, at each neck edge BO 3 sts once.

At the same time at each armhole edge BO 4 sts 3 times, then BO 4 (4, 4, 5, 5, 5) sts once—no sts rem.

front

Work as for back until waist incs have been completed, ending with the last RS waist inc row—81 (91, 101, 111, 121, 131, 141) sts; piece measures 13 (13½, 13½, 13½, 13¾, 14, 14)" (33 [34.5, 34.5, 34.5, 35, 35.5, 35.5] cm) from CO.

SHAPE NECK AND ARMHOLES

note: *Armhole shaping is introduced while neck shaping is in progress; read all the way through the foll section before proceeding so you do not accidentally work past the point where the armhole shaping begins.*

NEXT ROW: (WS) Work 38 (43, 48, 53, 58, 63, 68) sts in patt, p2tog through back loop (tbl), join a second ball of yarn, BO 1 st at center front, p2tog, work in patt to end—39 (44, 49, 54, 59, 64, 69) sts rem each side.

Working each side separately, dec 1 st at each neck edge every RS row 11 (13, 14, 14, 14, 14, 16) times, then every 4th row (i.e., every second RS row) 5 (5, 5, 6, 6, 7, 6) times—16 (18, 19, 20, 20, 21, 22) more sts removed at each neck edge.

At the same time when the piece measures 1" (2.5 cm) from front neck split and 14 (14½, 14½, 14½, 14¾, 15, 15)" (35.5 [37, 37, 37, 37.5, 38, 38] cm) from CO, shape armholes as foll: At each armhole edge, BO 3 (4, 5, 6, 6, 7, 7) sts once, then BO 3 sts once, then BO 2 sts 0 (1, 1, 1, 2, 3, 4) time(s), then dec 1 st 1 (1, 4, 7, 9, 10, 12) time(s)—7 (10, 14, 18, 22, 26, 30) sts removed at each armhole; 16 (16, 16, 16, 17, 17, 17) sts rem at each side when all neck and armhole shaping is complete.

Work even in patt until armholes measure 5½ (6, 6½, 7, 7, 7½, 7½)" (14 [15, 16.5, 18, 18, 19, 19] cm), ending with a WS row.

SHAPE SHOULDERS

At each armhole edge, BO 4 sts 3 times, then BO 4 (4, 4, 4, 5, 5, 5) sts once—no sts rem.

sleeves

With either cir needle, CO 46 (46, 50, 54, 58, 58, 62) sts.

SET-UP ROW: (WS) *P2, k2; rep from * to last 2 sts, p2.

Slipping the first st of every row, work in established rib until piece measures 1" (2.5 cm) from CO, ending with a RS row.

NEXT ROW: (WS) Sl 1, purl to end and *at the same time* dec 11 (11, 5, 9, 13, 3, 7) sts evenly spaced—35 (35, 45, 45, 45, 55, 55) sts rem.

NEXT ROW: (RS) Sl 1, k1, work Row 1 of **MANHEIM CHART** to the last 2 sts, k2.

NEXT ROW: Sl 1, p1, work Row 2 of chart to last 2 sts, p2.

Working 2 edge sts at each side as established, work rem sts in chart patt until piece measures 3½ (3½, 3½, 2¾, 2¾, 2¾, 2¾)" (9 [9, 9, 7, 7, 7, 7] cm) from CO, ending with a WS row.

INC ROW: (RS) Sl 1, k1, M1L, work in patt to last 2 sts, M1R, k2—2 sts inc'd.

Working new sts into established lace patt, [work 9 (9, 9, 7, 5, 5, 5)

rows even, then rep the inc row] 4 (4, 9, 6, 13, 16, 12) times—45 (45, 65, 59, 73, 89, 81) sts.

[Work 7 (7, 0, 5, 3, 0, 3) rows even, then rep the inc row] 5 (6, 0, 8, 5, 0, 7) times—55 (57, 65, 75, 83, 89, 95) sts; piece measures about 13 (14, 14¼, 14¼, 14¼, 14¼, 14½)" (33 [35.5, 36, 36, 36, 36, 37] cm) from CO.

Work even as established for 1½" (3.8 cm) more, ending with a WS row—piece measures about 14½ (15½, 15¾, 15¾, 15¾, 15¾, 16)" (37 [39.5, 40, 40, 40, 40, 40.5] cm from CO.

SHAPE CAP

BO 3 (4, 5, 6, 6, 7, 7) sts at the beg of the next 2 rows, then BO 3 sts at the beg of the foll 2 rows—43 (43, 49, 57, 65, 69, 75) sts rem.

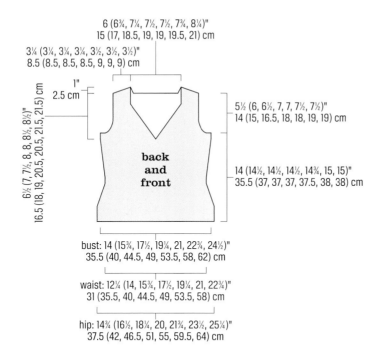

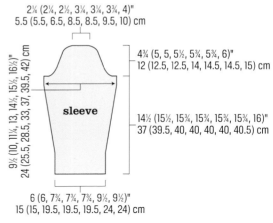

6 (6¾, 7¼, 7½, 7½, 7¾, 8¼)"
15 (17, 18.5, 19, 19, 19.5, 21) cm

3¼ (3¼, 3¼, 3¼, 3½, 3½, 3½)"
8.5 (8.5, 8.5, 8.5, 9, 9, 9) cm

1"
2.5 cm

5½ (6, 6½, 7, 7, 7½, 7½)"
14 (15, 16.5, 18, 18, 19, 19) cm

back and front

6½ (7, 7½, 8, 8, 8¼, 8½)"
16.5 (18, 19, 20.5, 20.5, 21.5, 21.5) cm

14 (14½, 14½, 14½, 14¾, 15, 15)"
35.5 (37, 37, 37, 37.5, 38, 38) cm

bust: 14 (15¾, 17½, 19¼, 21, 22¾, 24½)"
35.5 (40, 44.5, 49, 53.5, 58, 62) cm

waist: 12¼ (14, 15¾, 17½, 19¼, 21, 22¾)"
31 (35.5, 40, 44.5, 49, 53.5, 58) cm

hip: 14¾ (16½, 18¼, 20, 21¾, 23½, 25¼)"
37.5 (42, 46.5, 51, 55, 59.5, 64) cm

2¼ (2¼, 2½, 3¼, 3¼, 3¾, 4)"
5.5 (5.5, 6.5, 8.5, 8.5, 9.5, 10) cm

9½ (10, 11¼, 13, 14¼, 15½, 16½)"
24 (25.5, 28.5, 33, 37, 39.5, 42) cm

4¾ (5, 5, 5½, 5¾, 5¾, 6)"
12 (12.5, 12.5, 14, 14.5, 14.5, 15) cm

sleeve

14½ (15½, 15¾, 15¾, 15¾, 15¾, 16)"
37 (39.5, 40, 40, 40, 40, 40.5) cm

6 (6, 7¾, 7¾, 7¾, 9½, 9½)"
15 (15, 19.5, 19.5, 19.5, 24, 24) cm

BO 0 (2, 2, 2, 2, 2, 2) sts at the beg of the next 0 (2, 2, 2, 4, 6, 8) rows—43 (39, 45, 53, 57, 57, 59) sts rem.

[Work 2 rows even, then BO 1 st at beg of next 2 rows] 6 (8, 6, 6, 4, 4, 4) times, then BO 1 st at beg of the foll 8 (0, 8, 12, 20, 18, 18) rows—23 (23, 25, 29, 29, 31, 33) sts rem.

BO 2 sts at the beg of the next 2 rows, then BO 3 sts at the beg of the foll 2 rows—13 (13, 15, 19, 19, 21, 23) sts rem.

BO all sts.

finishing

Block to measurements. With yarn threaded on a tapestry needle, sew shoulder, side, and sleeve seams. Sew sleeve caps into armholes.

NECKBAND

With shorter cir needle, RS facing, and beg at center front, pick up and knit 1 st at base of V, 43 (44, 47, 50, 50, 53, 53) sts along right neck edge to shoulder seam, 40 (46, 48, 50, 50, 52, 56) sts across back neck, and 43 (44, 47, 50, 50, 53, 53) sts along left front neck edge from shoulder seam to base of V—127 (135, 143, 151, 151, 159, 163) sts total. Pm and join for working in rnds.

RND 1: K1, *p2, k2; rep from * to last 2 sts, p2.

RNDS 2–8: K1, k2tog, work in patt to last 2 sts, ssk—2 sts dec'd each rnd; 113 (121, 129, 137, 137, 145, 149) sts rem after Rnd 8.

BO all sts in patt.

Weave in loose ends.

Glossary

abbreviations

beg(s)	begin(s); beginning
bet	between
BO	bind off
cir	circular
cm	centimeter(s)
cn	cable needle
CO	cast on
cont	continue(s); continuing
dec(s)('d)	decrease(s); decreasing; decreased
dpn	double-pointed needles
foll	follow(s); following
g	gram(s)
inc(s)('d)	increase(s); increasing; increase(d)
k	knit
k1f&b	knit into the front and back of same stitch
k2tog	knit 2 stitches together
kwise	knitwise, as if to knit
m	marker(s)
mm	millimeter(s)
M1	make one (increase)
oz	ounce
p	purl
p1f&b	purl into front and back of same stitch
p2tog	purl 2 stitches together
patt(s)	pattern(s)
pm	place marker
psso	pass slipped stitch over
pwise	purlwise, as if to purl
rem	remain(s); remaining
rep	repeat(s); repeating
Rev St st	reverse stockinette stitch
rnd(s)	round(s)
RS	right side
sl	slip (slip 1 stitch purlwise unless otherwise indicated)
ssk	slip, slip, knit (decrease)
st(s)	stitch(es)
St st	stockinette stitch
tbl	through back loop
tog	together
WS	wrong side
wyb	with yarn in back
wyf	with yarn in front
yd	yard(s)
yo	yarnover
*****	repeat starting point
******	repeat all instructions between asterisks
( )	alternate measurements and/or instructions
[ ]	work instructions as a group a specified number of times

bind-offs

STANDARD BIND-OFF

Knit the first stitch, *knit the next stitch (two stitches on right needle), insert left needle tip into first stitch on right needle (**FIGURE 1**) and lift this stitch up and over the second stitch (**FIGURE 2**) and off the needle (**FIGURE 3**). Repeat from * until one stitch remains on the right needle. Cut the yarn, leaving a 6" (15 cm) tail, then pull on the loop of the last stitch until the tail comes free to secure the last stitch.

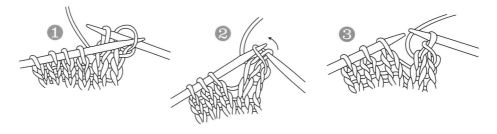

THREE-NEEDLE BIND-OFF

Place the stitches to be joined onto two separate needles and hold the needles parallel so that the right sides of knitting face together. Insert a third needle into the first stitch on each of two needles (**FIGURE 1**) and knit them together as one stitch (**FIGURE 2**), *knit the next stitch on each needle the same way, then use the left needle tip to lift the first stitch over the second and off the needle (**FIGURE 3**). Repeat from * until no stitches remain on the first two needles. Cut the yarn, leaving a 6" (15 cm) tail, then pull on the loop of the last stitch until the tail comes free to secure the last stitch.

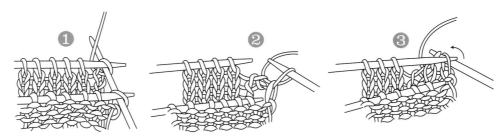

TUBULAR K1, P1 RIB BIND-OFF

Cut the yarn, leaving a tail three times the circumference of the knitting to be bound off, and thread the tail onto a tapestry needle.

STEP 1: Working from right to left, insert the tapestry needle purlwise (from right to left) through the first (knit) stitch (**FIGURE 1**) and pull the yarn through.

STEP 2: Bring the tapestry needle behind the knit stitch, then insert it knitwise (from left to right) into the second stitch (this will be a purl stitch; **FIGURE 2**), and pull the yarn through.

STEP 3: *Insert the tapestry needle into the first (knit) stitch knitwise and slip this stitch off the knitting needle (i.e., knit into the first st and slip it off the needle).

STEP 4: Bring the tapestry needle in front of the first (purl) stitch, then insert it purlwise into the second stitch (this will be a knit stitch; **FIGURE 3**) and pull the yarn through (i.e., purl into the second st and leave it on the needle).

STEP 5: Insert the tapestry needle into the first (purl) stitch purlwise and slip this stitch off the knitting needle (i.e., purl into the first st and slip it off the needle).

STEP 6: Bring the tapestry needle behind the knit stitch, then insert it knitwise into the second stitch (this will be a purl stitch; **FIGURE 4**), and pull the yarn through (i.e., knit into the second st and leave it on the needle).

Repeat from * until one stitch remains on the knitting needle. End by inserting the tapestry needle purlwise through the first (knit) stitch of the round (the first one slipped off the needle) and draw the yarn through, then purlwise through the last stitch and draw the yarn through.

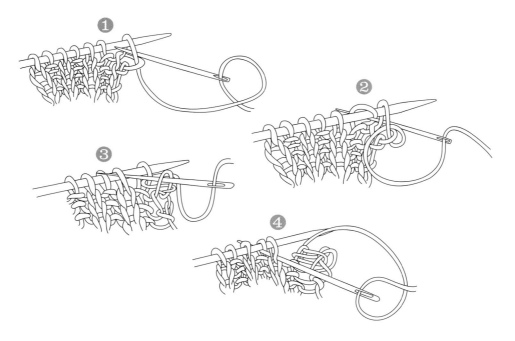

buttonhole

This method is worked over three stitches on a single row.

Bring the yarn to the front of the work, slip the next stitch purlwise, then return the yarn to the back. *Slip the next stitch, pass the second stitch over the slipped stitch and drop it off the needle. Repeat from * once more (**FIGURE 1**). Slip the last stitch on the right needle to the left needle and turn the work around. Bring the working yarn to the back, [insert the right needle between the first and second stitches on the left needle (**FIGURE 2**), draw up a loop and place it on the left needle] two times. Turn the work around. With the yarn in back, slip the first stitch and pass the extra cast-on stitch over it (**FIGURE 3**) and off the needle to complete the buttonhole.

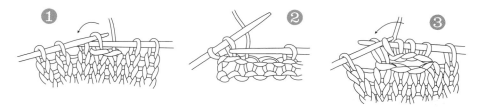

cast-ons

BACKWARD-LOOP CAST-ON

*Loop working yarn and place it on needle backward so that it doesn't unwind. Repeat from *.

EMILY OCKER'S CIRCULAR CAST-ON

Make a loose loop of working yarn. *Use a crochet hook to draw a loop of yarn through this loop, then draw another loop through the loop on the hook. Repeat from * for the desired number of stitches. Arrange stitches onto three or four double-pointed needles. After a few inches have been knitted, pull the loose end to tighten the initial loop and close the hole.

JUDY'S MAGIC CAST-ON

Leaving a 10" (25.5 cm) tail, drape the yarn over one needle, then hold a second needle parallel to and below the first and on top of the yarn tail (**FIGURE 1**).

Bring the tail to the back and the ball yarn to the front, then place the thumb and index finger of your left hand between the two strands so that the tail is over your index finger and the ball yarn is over your thumb (**FIGURE 2**). This forms the first stitch on the top needle.

*Continue to hold the two needles parallel and loop the finger yarn over the lower needle by bringing the lower needle over the top of the finger yarn (**FIGURE 3**), then bringing the finger yarn up from below the lower needle, over the top of this needle, and to the back between the two needles.

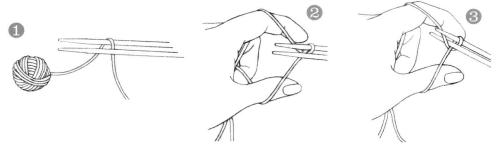

Point the needles downward, bring the bottom needle past the thumb yarn, then bring the thumb yarn to the front between the two needles and over the top needle (**FIGURE 4**).

Repeat from * until you have the desired number of stitches on each needle (**FIGURE 5**).

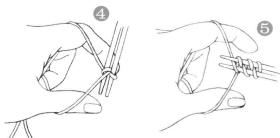

Remove both yarn ends from your left hand, rotate the needles like the hands of a clock so that the bottom needle is now on top and both strands of yarn are at the needle tip (**FIGURE 6**).

Using a third needle, knit half of the stitches from the top needle (**FIGURE 7**). There will now be the same number of stitches on two needles and twice that number of stitches on the bottom needle, and you're ready to work in rounds.

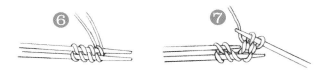

LONG-TAIL (CONTINENTAL) CAST-ON

Leaving a long tail (about ½" [1.3 cm] for each stitch to be cast on), make a slipknot and place it on right needle. Place the thumb and index finger of your left hand between the yarn ends so that the working yarn is around your index finger and the tail end is around your thumb, and secure the yarn ends with your other fingers. Hold your palm upwards, making a V of yarn (FIGURE 1). *Bring the needle up through the loop on your thumb (FIGURE 2), catch first strand around your index finger, and go back down through the loop on your thumb (FIGURE 3). Drop the loop off your thumb and, placing your thumb back in V configuration while tightening resulting stitch on needle (FIGURE 4). Repeat from * for the desired number of stitches.

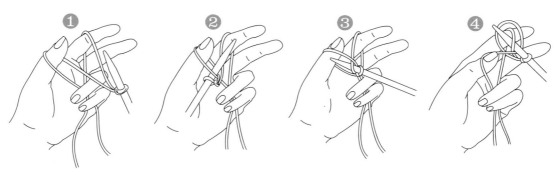

crochet

SINGLE CROCHET (SC)

Insert crochet hook into a stitch, *yarn over hook and draw through a loop, yarn over hook again (FIGURE 1), draw it through both loops on hook (FIGURE 2), and then insert the hook into the next stitch. Repeat from * for the desired number of stitches.

BACK-POST SINGLE CROCHET

Working from right to left, *insert crochet hook from back to front in the space before the next post (**FIGURE 1**) and then from front to back in the space after that post (**FIGURE 2**), yarn over hook, draw it through the two spaces—two loops on hook (**FIGURE 3**). Yarn over hook, draw it through the two loops already on the hook—one loop on hook (**FIGURE 4**). Repeat from * for the desired number of stitches.

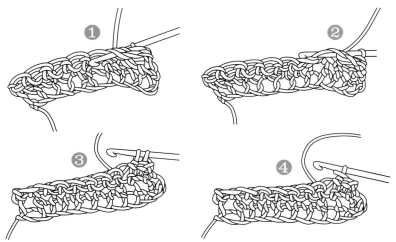

decreases

SLIP, SLIP, KNIT (SSK)

Slip two stitches individually knitwise (**FIGURE 1**), insert left needle tip into the fronts of these two slipped stitches, and use the right needle to knit them together through their back loops (**FIGURE 2**).

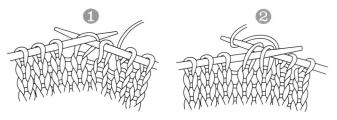

SLIP, SLIP, SLIP, KNIT (SSSK)

Slip three stitches individually knitwise (**FIGURE 1**), insert left needle tip into the fronts of these three slipped stitches, and use the right needle to knit them together through their back loops (**FIGURE 2**).

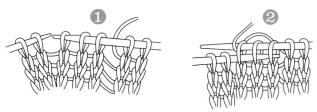

i-cord

Using two double-pointed needles, cast on the desired number of stitches (usually three to five). *Without turning the needle, slide the stitches to the other end of the needle, pull the yarn around the back of the work, then knit the stitches as usual. Repeat from * for the desired length.

increases

BAR INCREASE
KNITWISE (K1F&B)

Knit into a stitch but leave the stitch on the left needle (**FIGURE 1**), then knit through the back loop of the same stitch (**FIGURE 2**) and slip the original stitch off the needle (**FIGURE 3**).

PURLWISE (P1F&B)

Work as for the knitwise version, but purl into the front and back of the same stitch.

RAISED MAKE-ONE (M1) INCREASE

note: *Use the left slant if no direction of slant is specified.*

LEFT SLANT (M1L)

With left needle tip, lift the strand between the last knitted stitch and the first stitch on the left needle from front to back (**FIGURE 1**), then knit the lifted loop through the back to twist it (**FIGURE 2**).

To work this decrease purlwise (M1L purlwise), purl the lifted loop through the back.

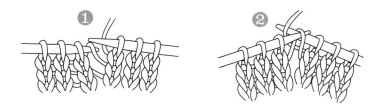

RIGHT SLANT (M1R)

Use the left needle tip to lift the strand between the needle tips from back to front (**FIGURE 1**), then knit the lifted loop through the front to twist it (**FIGURE 2**).

To work this decrease purlwise (M1R purlwise), purl the lifted loop through the front.

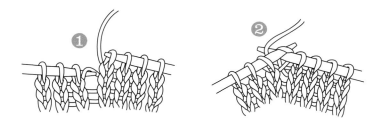

kitchener stitch

Arrange stitches on two needles so that there is the same number of stitches on each needle. Hold the needles parallel to each other with wrong sides of the knitting facing together. Allowing about ½" (1.3 cm) per stitch to be grafted, thread matching yarn on a tapestry needle. Work from right to left as follows:

STEP 1: Bring tapestry needle through the first stitch on the front needle as if to purl and leave the stitch on the needle (**FIGURE 1**).

STEP 2: Bring tapestry needle through the first stitch on the back needle as if to knit and leave that stitch on the needle (**FIGURE 2**).

STEP 3: Bring tapestry needle through the first front stitch as if to knit and slip this stitch off the needle, then bring the tapestry needle through the next front stitch as if to purl and leave this stitch on the needle (**FIGURE 3**).

STEP 4: Bring tapestry needle through the first back stitch as if to purl and slip this stitch off the needle, then bring the tapestry needle through the next back stitch as if to knit and leave this stitch on the needle (**FIGURE 4**).

Repeat Steps 3 and 4 until one stitch remains on each needle, adjusting the tension to match the rest of the knitting as you go. To finish, bring the tapestry needle through the front stitch as if to knit and slip this stitch off the needle, then bring the tapestry needle through the back stitch as if to purl and slip this stitch off the needle.

Insert the tapestry needle into the center of the last stitch worked, pull the yarn to the wrong side, and weave the tail into the purl bumps on the wrong side.

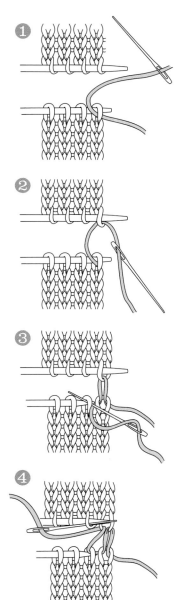

seams

INVISIBLE VERTICAL TO HORIZONTAL SEAM

Hold the pieces to be sewn together so that the bind-off edge of one piece abuts the selvedge of the other. *Bring threaded tapestry needle from back to front in the center V of a knit stitch just below the bind-off edge. Insert the needle under one or two bars between the first and second stitch in from the selvedge on the adjacent piece, then back down the front of same V exited before. Repeat from *, matching the tension of the the existing vertical stitches.

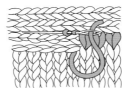

WHIPSTITCH

Hold the pieces to be sewn together so that the edges are even with each other. With yarn threaded on a tapestry needle, *insert needle through both layers from back to front, then bring the needle to the back. Repeat from *, working in a spiral motion and maintaining even tension.

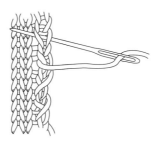

short-rows

SHORT-ROWS KNIT SIDE

Work to turning point, slip next stitch purlwise (**FIGURE 1**), bring the yarn to the front, then slip the same stitch back to the left needle (**FIGURE 2**), turn the work around and bring the yarn in position for the next stitch—one stitch has been wrapped, and the yarn is correctly positioned to work the next stitch. When you come to a wrapped stitch on a subsequent row, hide the wrap by working it together with the wrapped stitch as follows: Insert right needle tip under the wrap (from the front if wrapped stitch is a knit stitch (**FIGURE 3**); from the back if wrapped stitch is a purl stitch), then into the stitch on the needle, and work the stitch and its wrap together as a single stitch.

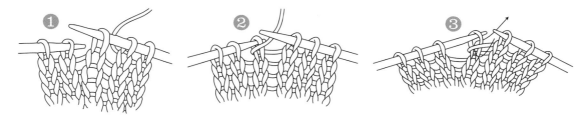

SHORT-ROWS PURL SIDE

Work to the turning point, slip the next stitch purlwise to the right needle, bring the yarn to the back of the work (**FIGURE 1**), return the slipped stitch to the left needle, bring the yarn to the front between the needles (**FIGURE 2**), then turn the work so that the knit side is facing—one stitch has been wrapped, and the yarn is correctly positioned to knit the next stitch. To hide the wrap on a subsequent purl row, work to the wrapped stitch, use the tip of the right needle to pick up the wrap from the back, place it on the left needle (**FIGURE 3**), then purl it together with the wrapped stitch.

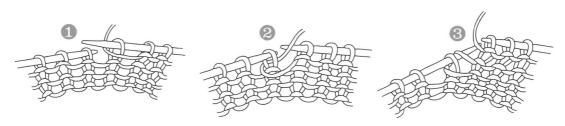

Sources for yarn

THE ALPACA YARN COMPANY
144 Roosevelt Ave., Bay #1
York, PA 17401
thealpacayarnco.com

BAAH!
baahyarn.com

BLUE SKY ALPACAS/SPUD & CHLOE
PO Box 88
Cedar, MN 55011
spudandchloe.com

CLASSIC ELITE YARNS
16 Esquire Rd., Unit 2
North Billerica, MA 01862
classiceliteyarns.com

DREAM IN COLOR
dreamincoloryarn.com

**FAIRMONT FIBERS/
MANOS DEL URUGUAY**
PO Box 2082
Philadelphia, PA 19103
fairmountfibers.com

IMPERIAL YARN
92462 Hinton Rd.
Maupin, OR 97037
imperialyarn.com

JUNIPER MOON FARM
fiberfarm.com

MADELINETOSH
7517 Benbrook Pkwy.
Benbrook, TX 76126
madelinetosh.com

MALABRIGO
malabrigoyarn.com

QUINCE AND COMPANY
quinceandco.com

WESTMINSTER FIBERS/REGIA
165 Ledge St.
Nashua, NH 03060
in Canada:
10 Roybridge Gate, Ste. 200
Vaughan, ON L4H 3M8
westminsterfibers.com

SWANS ISLAND
231 Atlantic Hwy.
Northport, ME 04849
swansislandcompany.com

SWEET GEORGIA
110-408 East Kent Ave. S.
Vancouver, BC
Canada V5X 2X7
sweetgeorgiayarns.com

UNIVERSAL YARN
5991 Caldwell Business Park Dr.
Harrisburg, NC 28075
universalyarn.com

Index

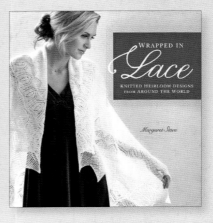
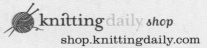
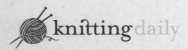